FOLKTALES OF THE SCOTTISH BORDERS

The Rookhope Ride

FOLKTALES OF THE SCOTTISH BORDERS

◆

William & Susan Platt

SENATE

Folktales of the Scottish Borders

First published in 1919 as *Stories of the Scottish Border*
by George G. Harrap & Co, London

This edition published in 1999 by Senate,
an imprint of Senate Press Limited,
34 York Street, Twickenham,
Middlesex TW1 3LJ, United Kingdom

3 5 7 9 10 8 6 4 2

ISBN 1 85958 542 6

Printed and bound in the UK by
Mackays of Chatham plc, Chatham, Kent

Contents

Illustrations

In liquid murmurs Yarrow sings
Her reminiscent tune
Of bygone Autumn, bygone Springs,
And many a leafy June.

No more the warning beacons gleam
Upon the silent hills;
The far back years are years of dream—
Now peace the valley fills.

No more the reivers down the vale
On raid and foray ride;
No more is heard the widow's wail
O'er those who fighting died.

When morning dawns with all its joys
Then from the meadows rise
A hundred throbbing hearts to voice
Their anthems to the skies.

When noontide sleeps where brackens wave,
Ere shadows yet grow long,
No sound awakes the echoes save
The Yarrow's pensive song.

And when the eve, with calm delight,
Betokens night is nigh,
Beneath the first star's tender light
Is heard the owlet's cry.

While Yarrow's liquid cadence swells
By meadow, moor, and hill,
At morn or noon or eve there dwells
A mournful memory still.

W. CUTHBERTSON.

Stories of The Scottish Border

Introduction

I.—THE CHARACTER OF THE BORDERS

THE district called the Border is one of the most interesting in Great Britain. It consists of that part of England that is nearest Scotland, and that part of Scotland that is nearest England, mainly the counties of Northumberland, Cumberland, Berwickshire, Roxburghshire, and Dumfriesshire.

The country is very picturesque and highly romantic. It abounds in great rolling, breezy hills, with swift streamlets or "burns" running down their sides to swell the rushing rivers. No part of our island has more beautiful valleys than those of the Border.

This bold, rough district, well adapted to defence, and situated also just where the island of Great Britain is almost at its narrowest, became, after many a struggle, the boundary between England and Scotland. The character of the country was suited to the rearing of hardy Moorland sheep and cattle; its inhabitants therefore were a tough, open-air race of men, strong, strapping fellows, fearless riders, always ready for an adventure, especially if it meant a fight.

In those days of Border strife there was hardly such a thing as international justice, that is to say, the people of one nation were not very particular as to what they did to people of another nation; therefore these bold, hardy Border men, Englishmen and Scot alike, were fond of creeping across the boundary to steal the cattle of their neighbours. Men devoted to such raids were called "Freebooters" or "Mosstroopers," the name "Moss" being given in the North Country to boggy tracts that lie about the hill-sides.

So it happened that the Border was in a perpetual state of petty warfare, conducted, it is true, with a certain amount of good-will and a rough approach to chivalry, and with the concurrence of the powerful Border nobles of both nations, who often played an important part therein. At times these raids developed into important warlike expeditions, when a fierce noble, or even a king, had some reckless game to play. Hence, among the ballads which give us so vivid an account of Border strife, we find descriptions not only of the minor doings of picturesque sheep-stealers, but also of pitched battles such as Chevy Chase and Homildon Hill.

The union of England and Scotland in 1603 naturally put an end to all the former excuses for raiding, and therefore terminated the true Freebooter period. After this, despite one or two belated attempts, such as Elliot's big raid in 1611, sheep-stealing ceased to be looked upon as an honourable calling, and became mere thieving. The men who would have raided one another's farms in 1602 became friendly neighbours after the Border Commission of 1605. There had been little malice in their former freebooting. Both sides were of one race; and they had the pleasure of finding that their lands went up greatly in value in consequence of the Border peace.

To-day, the Border presents scenes of peaceful cattle-farming. But Romance is still in the air, hangs about the fine, breezy moorlands and beautiful dales, and is seen clearly in the faces of the healthy Border-folk. A holiday at any Border farm would prove a most enjoyable one. There are wonderful Roman remains, for here it was that the Romans built their wall; there are castles of the Border barons; the views are wide and grand; the river-valleys are unmatched for beauty, and delightful wild flowers are plentiful, chief among which are fox-gloves, the giant wild Canterbury Bells, the handsome North Country wild geranium, several interesting kinds of wild orchids, and a variety of others too numerous to mention. Last, but not least, it is often possible in the evenings to see the farmers' sons engaged in friendly wrestling in the meadows, when we can realise that these great manly fellows are of the same vigorous race that kept the Borders lively a few centuries ago.

II.—A BRIEF HISTORY OF THE BORDER

Before dealing in detail with the stirring stories of Border history and legend, to retell which is the purpose of this book, we will first inquire—What is it that settles exactly the position of the border-line between two countries? To find the answer we must think what happens when a country is invaded.

If the invaders are stronger than the people whom they attack, they go on thrusting back their foes till these reach some strong position where, by the aid of mountain, river, or marsh, they are able, at any rate for a time, to hold their own. Thus, a border-line is always determined by some natural feature of the country which gives the defenders an advantage.

The attackers will not always operate from the same locality, and the defenders will not always fall back in the same direction; the two sides, also, will vary in power from time to time. For these reasons a border-line, especially in the old fighting days, was often altered.

When the Romans invaded Britain they gradually conquered the southern part of it, but they could not subdue the wilder north; one of their boundary lines was drawn from the Solway to the Tyne; then they fought their way further north and their next definite boundary was a line running from the Forth to the Clyde. Along each of these boundaries they built a great wall, and to this day parts of these Roman walls remain. But it is worth noting that neither of these wall border-lines stands upon the present border, one being all in England and the other all in Scotland.

When the Romans left Britain, called back to defend their own native land from invasion, there followed a brief period for which we have no definite record of events in this island. This is the period of King Arthur, and none can say how much is true in the Arthurian legends.

But history begins to become clear again about the time that the Angles came in their ships across the North Sea, bent on conquest. They landed on all the natural harbours of the east coast, driving the Britons back and taking the land for themselves. The fact that they landed on the East and drove the Britons westward, leads us to think that sooner or later a boundary would have been formed dividing the island into the east side (for the Angles) and the west side (for the Britons).

Now that is exactly what did happen. The border-lines were nowhere like the present ones. The northern kingdom of the Angles reached to the Forth, where these people founded Edinburgh (Edwin's burgh). On the west the Britons had sway in Cornwall (Corn-Walles), Wales, Cumbria (which stretched from the Mersey to the Solway), and Strathclyde (from the Solway to the Clyde). North of the Forth was the country of the Picts; while the Scots were a race recently come from Ireland, and they only owned what we now call Argyleshire, and the islands lying near to it. Not one inch of the present Border was at that day in the border-line!

Of the various races that lay round about where the Border now is, the Northumbrians seemed at first to be the strongest. The capital of their kingdom was Bamburgh, a place still famous for its castle, though to-day it is not important enough to have a railway station! But it still looks very picturesque on the wild coast, with the Farne Islands, the first seat of Northumbrian Christianity, in the near distance.

Ambition had much to do with the downfall of Northumbria. The famous King Eadbert would not rest content till he had scaled Dumbarton, the capital of Strathclyde. This was to his career what the march to Moscow was to Napoleon's, for, though Eadbert got safely to Dumbarton (756) his army was cut to pieces in getting back again. The Northumbrians seem to have lost some of their northern lands, for they moved their capital further south, to the old Roman city of Corbridge which stood on the Tyne just where the delightful country town of that name stands to-day.

In 844 a king of the Scots, named Kenneth MacAlpin, became (we don't quite know how) king of the Picts also, joining two strong races under one ruler, and thus was powerful enough to give great trouble to the weakened kingdom of Northumbria. He several times led his army through Lothian, the district belonging to the Angles between the Forth and the Tweed, but was never quite able to conquer it. It is important to remember that up to that date Lothian had never belonged to Scotland.

The appearance of the Danes added to the confusion of those restless days. For some few years it was doubtful whether Scot, Dane, or Angle would get the best of it in Northumbria. But at last the genius of Athelstan of Wessex revived the power of the Angles over the whole of that large part of the island which they had settled, right up to the Forth itself. Edinburgh was still English in 957, and the border-line was still very far from the present one. But there was no longer a king of Northumbria; only an earl, who was subject to the will of the West-Saxon kings.

This fact of the dominance of the West Saxons, whose capital was far to the south at Winchester, must have added to the weakness of the Northumbrian border. By the year 963 the Scots had conquered Edinburgh, and it was now never again to return to English rule. Before very long the whole of Lothian had passed under Scottish control; but it was not yet held to be part of Scotland. Nor must it be thought that this conquest of Lothian fixed the border-line in its present position, for the king of the Scots was at that time ruler over Cumberland, which had never yet been English and was all that was left of the old British kingdom of Cumbria.

Frontier wars with varying successes between Scot, Angle, and Dane mark the stormy history of this time. The power of Cnut held back the Scotch attempts upon Nothumberland; but during a lull in the wars the grandson of the Scottish king married the sister of Earl Siward, and received as her dowry twelve towns in the valley of the Tyne, an astonishingly imprudent arrangement.

At the time of the battle of Hastings, the earldom of Northumberland was so far distant from Winchester as to be somewhat out of the control of the King of England; the power of the Scottish kings threatened it; they held twelve towns in Tynedale, and Cumberland was a part of Scotland. The Northumbrians refused to accept William the Conqueror as their king; and had they been able to make good their refusal, they must sooner or later have been conquered by the Scots, and the border-line between England and Scotland would then most probably have been formed by the Tees, the mountain boundary of Westmoreland, and Morecambe Bay.

But William was not a king to be played with. He reduced Northumberland to subjection and carried his army into Scotland as far as the river Tay, where he forced the King of Scotland to admit that he, William, was his overlord.

Notwithstanding this humiliation, when King William returned to Winchester, the Scots several times went back to their favourite amusement of raiding unhappy Northumberland.

One of these invasions took place in the reign of William Rufus (1093), who went north in person. He doubtless recognised the fact that owing to the Scots possessing Cumberland they were in the strong position of being able to attack Northumberland on two sides. He took Cumberland by force of arms, and thus for the first time it became a part of England (the word "Cumberland" means the land of the Cumbrians or Welsh, a Saxon form of the Welsh word Cymry).

Rufus rebuilt the strong fortress of Carlisle to defend

his new border at its weakest corner. For the most part this border is excellently protected by the natural rampart of the wild Cheviot Hills, and is in every way as good a border as could be devised. It runs in a fairly straight line from south-west to north-east, across a narrow part of the island.

But although this border-line proved to be a permanent one, it must not be thought that it remained undisputed. The times were rough, and hardy fighting folk lived on the Border. They had many grounds for quarrel, and took advantage of them all. For one thing, the exact boundary of North Cumberland was never quite defined till 1552; up to which year there was a tract of land between the rivers Esk and Sark, which was claimed by both countries, and therefore called the "Debateable Land." Then the Scots maintained that they were overlords of Northumberland, while the English kings cherished the notion that they were overlords of the whole island of Britain, and the wild spirits on both sides were always ready to fight.

Out of this fighting spirit sprung the stirring history of the Border, which forms the theme of the deathless Ballads, the stories of which it is now our purpose to retell.

III.—WHAT THE BORDER NAMES TELL US

Many a name holds a meaning wrapt up within itself like a nut in its shell. For instance, "Edinburgh" is a Saxon name—Edwin's burgh—and the word tells us that this noble city, though now the capital of Scotland, was originally founded by and belonged to a Saxon king of Northumbria. The Highlanders, in their own Gaelic language, called it Dunedin. This has the same signification as Edinburgh, but, like most

Gaelic names, it is arranged in the reverse order to that in which an English name is generally put together. "Dun" means burgh, "Edin" is Edwin. This is the same Dun that we have in "Dundee," which means the burgh on the Tay, and might be translated as "Tayburgh." "Dumbarton" means the burgh of the Britons, and teaches us another notable lesson, namely, how far north in the old times the British influence extended. For "British" in this case means "Welsh." Nowadays we associate the Welsh with Wales only. Formerly there must have been a numerous colony of Welsh in Scotland, as the name "Dumbarton" testifies, as also many Scottish family names. The great name of Wallace itself, for instance, suggests such an origin, for "Wallace" is merely a corrupt form of the word "Welsh," and proves that the great national hero was of Welsh extraction. Then "Cumberland"—Cymry land—means the land of the Welsh, or Cymry, as they call themselves. The county of Cumberland did not really belong to the English till the time of William Rufus. The first syllable of "Carlisle" denotes a Celtic fortified town, and must be compared with the first syllable of "Carnarvon."

The presence of the Roman wall is shown in many names in Northumberland, such as "Wallsend," "Walltown," "Wallridge," "Heddon-on-the-Wall," "Wallhouses," and "Thirlwall."

For a very interesting instance of what a name tells us we may leave the Border for a moment and consider why the northernmost part of Scotland is called "Sutherland." It must have been so named by people living in the Orkney and Shetland isles, of a different race from the Scotch—that is, Norse settlers in those islands.

With regard to surnames, how many stop to think that "Oliphant" is merely a form of "elephant," and was originally an allusion to a big, burly ancestor? "Grant," which is the same as "grand," must also have been once applied to one who was a giant in size. The Frazers somehow got their name from the French word for a strawberry, *fraise.* The odd-looking "Scrymgeour" means simply a scrimmager or skirmisher. "Turnbull" recalls one who turned the bull at a bull-baiting. The well-known "Gladstains" or "Gladstone" has nothing to do with "glad," but is from "glede," an old word for the kite, and commemorates some stone where these birds frequented. "Buccleuch" is from the killing of a buck in a cleugh or ravine.

The Christian names of the Borderers are full of life and local colour, and differ much from those of Southern England. "Barthram" is the northern form of "Bertram," "Nigel" of "Neil," "Jellon" of "Julian," "Ringan" of "Ninian." It was the general custom to abbreviate Christian names or use them in the diminutive form, as is constantly the practice in these Border ballads. "Hobbie" stands for "Halbert," a fine old name which must not be confused with "Albert." "Dandie" or "Dandrie" is "Andrew," "Eckie" is "Hector," "Lammie" is "Lambert," "Lennie" is "Leonard." "Adam" becomes, in the familiar form, "Aicky," "Christian" becomes "Christy," "Gilbert" becomes "Gibby."

Another peculiarity of the ballads is the regular recurrence of such phrases as "the Laird's Jock," "the Laird's Wat," "Ringan's Wat," etc. These expressions mean, "John the son of the Laird," "Walter the son of the Laird," "Walter the son of Ringan or Ninian."

Chapter I

Bamburgh and its Coast

THE little town of Bamburgh has two striking features—the great castle upon its stern rock, and the wild coast-line at its feet where dash the storms of the North Sea.

To-day it is not important enough to have a railway station of its own; yet once it was the capital of the great Saxon kingdom of Northumbria. Its original name was Bebbanburgh, so called after Queen Bebba; of its Saxon fortress hardly a trace remains, the present building being partly the old Norman castle, with repairs and additions of a later date. The ancient pile has a strength, dignity, and grandeur which accords well with its truly noble situation.

The North Saxons in choosing such a spot for their capital showed a very evident desire to keep in touch with the sea. Over the sea they had come; and over the sea would come both friends and enemies. Many a meeting of both friend and foe has taken place at Bamburgh!

Perhaps the fiercest of the enemies was Ragnar of the hairy-breeches, a famous viking who plundered, ravaged, and burnt without mercy. These vikings, powerful men and fearless sea-rovers, were a standing terror to Northumbria. Men with frames and muscles strong as iron; at home both on the sea and on the battle-field;

fair-haired, blue-eyed men, guarded by helmet, breastplate, and shield, armed with heavy weapons, because at that date the art of the smith was not equal to making them sharp, light, and strong at once. So these mighty warriors hewed their way through the field of battle with great strokes, and when their foes fled in terror, the vikings took back to their ships all the treasure they could find, and away they went across the sea again. But with all their fierceness they loved poetry (wild war-poetry, most of it) and they loved their strong, brave women.

Ragnar was a thorough viking. He loved fighting, and his handsome wife, and the battle songs he made. But the Saxons had no cause to love him, and when his ship ran aground near Jarrow, they bound him and cast him into a pit of snakes, and watched him slowly die. The viking had no fear of death. He sang as he lay there, of his life and his deeds—of the great banquets he had given to the wolves and the vultures and the fierce battles he had won, spreading the terrors of his name from the Orkneys to the Mediterranean ; of his beautiful wife and strong sons, and of how they would avenge him ; and of how Woden, the lord of all warriors, was calling him to his Hall.

Many a battle has been fought on that wild coast since Ragnar died ; much history has been made thereabouts, and many legends have attached themselves to Bamburgh. Like most famous places, it had its own special dragon, the " Laidly Worm " or loathsome serpent of the ancient ballad.

" For seven miles east, and seven miles west,
And seven miles north and south,
No blade of grass or corn would grow,
So venomous was her mouth ! "

And yet, when the gallant knight gave her "kisses three," she changed at once into a beautiful lady!

But despite its castle, its battles, and its legends, Bamburgh slowly declined in importance. As the capital of Northumbria it had been one of the chief towns in England. But the gallant Northumbria of the Saxons was more open to enemies than any other part of the country; Cumbrians were on the west and Scots on the north, and this was of all Saxon kingdoms the most exposed to the ravages of the Danes. From the capital of a kingdom it became the capital of a county (Bamburghshire), returning two members to Parliament in the reign of Edward I.; but it grew of less and still less importance, till at last it was known only to the student of history. It shared this fate with Lindisfarne, called Holy Island, once the Canterbury of the North, on whose rocky shores still stand the ruins of the fine Norman cathedral which took the place of the old Saxon one. Lindisfarne and Bamburgh—neighbours, divided only by a narrow belt of sea—two names that conjure up vivid pictures of romantic history. Yet suddenly, early in the nineteenth century, the great deed of a splendid heroine lent new glory to the wild, sea-girt town.

Grace Darling was born at Bamburgh in 1817, in a cottage on the south side of the village street, which can still be seen to-day. Her father became keeper of the lighthouse on the Langstone, a rocky islet five miles from the coast, guarding ships from the dangerous Farne Islands, a group of iron-bound rocks where sea-birds dwell. In the early morning of September 7, 1838, during the raging of a most terrible storm, she heard the crash of a ship dashed upon the rocks, and anguished cries; as soon as dawn enabled them to see, the girl and her father made out the dark outline of the wreck, and the miserable forms of the mariners crouching on rocks from which the rising tide would sweep them inevitably to death. With superb heroism Grace and her father pushed their small boat into the furious waters, and after strenuous and dauntless efforts, always at the peril of their own lives, they saved the whole ship's company, nine souls in all. So fierce was the storm that it was three days before a boat dared take them from the Langstone to the mainland.

The roar of approbation which greeted her from the whole country found her as modest as she was brave. But for all her courage, this noble girl was not strong. She died four years later, and lies buried at Bamburgh, within sound of the sea. And the Langstone is known to-day as "Grace Darling's Island," and the tomb of the brave girl rouses sweeter memories than the frowning fortress of Bamburgh.

Chapter II

Athelstan at Vinheath

FAMOUS among the old Norse sea-rovers was Egil, son of Skallagrim. In the course of his many voyages, he visited all the lands between the White Sea and the Bay of Biscay, and when at last he settled down in his Iceland home, where he lived on till well past the age of eighty, he loved to gather his children and grandchildren around him by the fireside during the long Icelandic winter, and to tell the story of his adventures. He was a true Norseman, fond of the sea and the fight, fond of his wife and children, fond of song, at which he was highly skilled. His songs and his stories of adventure were listened to with eagerness, and they were repeated after him, and were at last written down, probably between one hundred and fifty and two hundred years after his death. Books were scarce in those days, and stories were treasured and faithfully re-told. So this story of Egil was probably written out very much in the simple, vigorous style in which the old warrior would have told it to his grandchildren, as they listened to him with wide-open, wondering eyes. And as the old man had taken part in an early battle between Saxon-English and Scots, upon the Border, we have here a fine picture of how fights were fought in the reign of King Athelstan.

Egil was speaking to Icelandic children who knew

little about England, so he began by telling how in the days when Harold Fairhair was king of Norway, Alfred the Great was the first supreme king over all England. When Alfred died he was succeeded by his son Edward, who was followed by Athelstan the Victorious. In Egil's day Athelstan was young and had but just been made king, and many chieftains, who had kept quiet before, now thought that the time had come when they could do as they pleased again. But Athelstan meant to show them that he too could rule England strongly and wisely.

These were the days of brute force, and the king had first to get an army together. Besides his own English folk, many roving Norsemen came to take his pay, and among the number were Egil and his elder brother Thorolf, with their men. They saw the king himself, who received them well. Athelstan was a good Christian, known as the Faithful, and he desired that Thorolf and Egil should submit to be marked with the Cross, that they might take their place by his Christian soldiers without quarrel. This they agreed to, and the king gave them command over three hundred men. Now Olaf the Red was king in Scotland. His father was a Scot, but his mother was a Dane of the family of Ragnar with-the-hairy-breeches, that savage old viking. Northumberland, which in those days extended to the Humber, and included York as its chief city, was half-full of Danes, and King Olaf wished to claim it for his own, and add it to Scotland.

Athelstan had set Earl Alfgeir and Earl Gudrek to rule Northumberland and defend it from the Scots. But Olaf of Scotland came south with his mighty host; there was a fierce battle; Earl Gudrek was slain and Earl Alfgeir fled. When Athelstan heard of the triumph of

Olaf, he began at once to march northward with all the men he could get together; but he was yet young, and some of the treacherous earls, hearing that Olaf had so far been victor, deserted King Athelstan. Chief among these traitors were Earl Hring and Earl Adils, who should have been in the very front of the English army, but who basely went over to the Scots. Thus Olaf's host became exceeding great, greater by far than the English army.

Then Athelstan called together his captains and his counsellors; Egil was there, and heard all the grave talk as to what should be done. At last a plan was made that all thought good, and this is what followed.

First, messengers were sent to King Olaf, saying that King Athelstan would meet him in fair fight at Vinheath by Vinwood, in Northumberland, where he would mark out the field of battle with rods of hazel. He who won the battle should be king over all England. The armies should meet a week hence, and whichever was first on the ground should wait a week for the other. King Olaf should bide quiet, and not harry the land till the battle was ended. North of the heath was a town; there King Olaf stayed, for there he could best get provisions for his army. But some of his men he sent to the heath, to view it.

The hazel-poles were already set up on the large level plain. A river was on one side, and a wood was on the other. And where river and wood were nearest to one another, there King Athelstan's tents were pitched.

Many tents there were, but the front line of tents stood high, so that the Scots could not see how many were behind. Every third tent was empty, but many men were sleeping on the grass in the open, so that the

Scots might think that the English had a large army there. Every day more English troops came in, and when the time was come that was fixed for the battle, English envoys went to the King of the Scots asking if there need be the great fight and bloodshed that threatened ; if Olaf would go peaceably home, Athelstan would give him a shilling of silver for every plough that ploughed in England. The Scots took counsel together and said they must have more than this. Then the messengers begged a three days' truce to consider this. On the third day they came again, saying that King Athelstan would give what he offered before and also to the Scottish army a silver shilling for every freeman soldier, a silver mark for every lesser officer, a gold mark for every captain, and five gold marks for every earl. But the Scots asked not only for this, but also for Northumberland to be yielded to them. Then the English messengers answered that Scottish messengers must ride back with them, to take the answer from Athelstan himself.

Now the truth is this : that the Scottish king had taken Athelstan by such surprise that he needed time to get his men together ; all these messages were but a trick to gain time till the king should come up himself with all the men he could gather. When, therefore, the messengers rode up to King Athelstan, he had but just arrived on the scene of battle. And when he heard the message he said : " Tell King Olaf this, that I will give him leave to return to Scotland safely if only he give back all he has unjustly taken from this land, and if he own himself my under-king, holding Scotland for me and at my behest."

This proud answer made the Scottish messengers at once see what had been going on. So they hastened back to their king to tell him how they had been received and what the meaning of it was.

When the Scots found that the English had thus outwitted them, they took counsel together in some anger. Earl Adils, he who had deserted the English, said that he and his brother, Earl Hring, would that very night make a surprise attack; if it succeeded, well and good; if not, then they could easily withdraw, and the main battle could begin in the morning. This the King of Scots held to be good advice.

So the two traitor earls and their men moved southward under cover of the darkness. But Thorolf the Norseman was used to the ways of war, and his sentries were alert and blew a great war-blast on their horns. And thus the fight began.

Thorolf was armed with a massy halberd that stood taller than a man; broad was its blade and thick its socket, and it ended in a four-edged spike. He had a strong sword by his side and a big, heavy shield on his left arm; he had a helmet but no shirt of mail. His brother Egil was armed in much the same way. The Norsemen's standard was borne by Thorfid the strong.

Next to the Norsemen, in the first rank also, was the division led by Earl Alfgeir, he who had once before fled from the Scots. King Athelstan gave him this chance to redeem himself. Now when the first onslaught of the Scots took place, Earl Adils came against Earl Alfgeir, while Earl Hring came against the Norsemen.

And now the battle began. The two traitor earls urged on their men, who charged with spirit. The fight was fierce, and soon Alfgeir gave ground; this made the foe press on the fiercer, and before long Alfgeir was in full flight. He avoided the town where Athelstan was, and fled night and day to the coast, where he took ship out of the country he had served so ill.

Adils did not dare to pursue him far, for fear of being himself cut off from his friends. So he returned to help his brother Hring against the Norsemen. Thorolf, like a true general, saw the danger of this, and at once told Egil to turn aside with half their force to prevent Adils from joining his brother. The Norsemen fought a grand fight, but were badly outnumbered, and the battle seemed to be going against them. Then Thorolf became furious. Disdainful of life, he cast his shield behind his back, grasped his great halberd with both hands, and sprang forward, hacking down all who opposed him. Straight for Hring's standard he went, nothing could stop him. He slew the standard-bearer, cut through the standard-pole, and with a mighty stroke thrust his halberd right through the body of Hring, the traitor earl, and lifted him up in the air that all might see that he was slain. Then Adils and the rest of the men fled to the wood, and thus ended the first part of the fight. More was to come on the morrow.

At dawn next day King Athelstan came forward with his main army. He had heard of the great deeds of the brothers Thorolf and Egil; most courteously he thanked them, and said that he would always reckon them as his friends. Then with his captains he made his plans for the battle. Egil he put in command of the front ranks of his men, and Thorolf he set aside to face those of the Scots who might charge the English in loose array.

"For this is the way of the Scots," he said; "they dash to and fro, rush forward and hither and thither, and are dangerous except to a commander who is both wary and bold."

Egil at Vinheath

Egil said, " I would rather that Thorolf and I were near together " ; but Thorolf answered, " As the king commands, so will we do."

The battle began, and soon waged furiously. Thorolf and his men pressed forward along the woodside, hoping to take the enemy on the flank. Now, unknown to him, Adils and his followers were hiding among the trees, and of a sudden Adils sprang out and smote him down. Thorfid, too, the brave standard-bearer, was pressed back, but rallied the men, who fought desperately.

The Scots had raised a great shout at the fall of Thorolf, and this was heard by Egil, who, when he saw the standard forced back, feared that his brother was dead, for Thorolf had never drawn back from any foe. So with a fierce cry Egil hacked his way through to that part of the field, and when he learnt the truth from his men, he never rested till he had slain Adils with his own hand.

The followers of Adils then fled, and Egil and the Norsemen hewed their way through the flank of the Scottish force towards the place where King Olaf's standard was. Noting this, King Athelstan, that wary general, caused his own standard to be set forward and all his army to attack at once. Fierce and furious was the fight, and great was the slaughter. King Olaf was slain, with great numbers of his men, and the rest fled in confusion. The English victory was complete.

As soon as Athelstan saw that victory was his, he left the pursuit to his captains and hastened to the town to make his arrangements. Egil pursued far and fiercely, and when at last he came back to the battlefield his first thought was for his dead brother. Worn out though he was, he would take no rest until he had buried the warrior with full honours, with his arms and his raiment; and before the sad farewell was said Egil clasped a gold bracelet on both of Thorolf's wrists to show his deep love. Then they buried the hero deep and put a high cairn of stones over him.

Then one last tribute Egil paid to his brother, the greatest of them all. Among these old Norse warriors there existed a great love of song; the great fighters strove also to be great song-makers, and Egil was famous above most for this power. The Norsemen's poems had not rhymes like ours; they had short vigorous lines, and in each pair of lines three of the important words had to begin with the same letter. Wild strong chants they were. This is the song that Egil sang at the burial of his brother, Thorolf Skallagrimsson:—

> "The halberd of the hero
> Hewed down the foe before him;
> Then in the brunt of battle
> Was spilt brave Thorolf's blood.
> The grass is green on Vinheath
> Where sleeps my great-souled brother;
> But death, in doubled sorrow,
> Our doleful hearts must bear."

When Egil got to the town he found the king and his army making merry over their victory at a huge feast. The courteous king saw Egil and bade him come and sit near to him. The king watched the burly Norseman, who was tall, with broad shoulders, a powerful head and mighty strength; but now his head was bent forward, and he kept his sword across his knees, and now and again half drew it and then clashed it back into its scabbard like a man who fights with heavy thoughts. He ate little and drank less. Then King Athelstan, watchful and courteous, took a gold ring from his arm, and placing it on his sword-point, handed it thus to where Egil sat. At this mark of honour the Norseman's face grew brighter. Then the king sent round his own horn for Egil to drink; so he drank to the king and sang a verse of wild poetry in his praise, made on the spur of the moment; and with this the king was much pleased.

Then the king sent also for two chests full of silver, and said to Egil:—

"These chests carry to thy father; it is fitting that King Athelstan make him some gift for the loss of his son. And do thou stay with me long, and I will give thee honour and dignity."

Thus the great king in kindness and courtesy did what he could to soothe the grief of the warrior; and Egil stayed the winter with Athelstan, but when the summer came he wished to go back to his own people. But he had much respect for King Athelstan, and ere he bade him farewell he made a long poem to his glory.

From the Song of Egil Skallagrimsson, to the Glory of King Athelstan.

"See how the kingly warrior,
Land-warder, battle-wakener,
Smites even to the earth
The earls who rise against him!
Glad is now Northumberland,
This the king she needed,
Wise and bold of race and blood,
Dauntless in the battle-field!"

Many were the verses of this stirring song; and after each came the refrain:—

"Scottish hills where reindeer roam
Own the rule of Athelstan!"

The king gave Egil two heavy gold rings and a handsome cloak that he himself had worn; then the Norseman sailed away, for always near to his heart was the welfare of his dead brother's wife and child. Yea, for the rest of his long life he loved this child even as he loved his own.

Chapter III

Monks and Minstrels

THE wild Borderland was the scene of the labours of many of the first great Christian leaders. Where the arts of war were so much practised, it was needful that the arts of peace should flourish also. Great was the influence, even in the wildest times, of these able, serious, devoted leaders of early religious thought, men like Ninian and Kentigern.

Christianity first came into Britain in Roman times, and some of the Britons were converted. After the Romans quitted the country, King Arthur was the leader of the Christian Britons, and he is said to have fought with the pagan Britons, the pagan Picts, the pagan Saxons, who had begun their invasions, and the disorderly soldiers of various races, probably pagans whom the Romans left behind along the wall.

In due time the fight developed into a struggle between Christian Britons and pagan Saxons, and then the Saxons themselves began to accept the new religion. Oswald, a Northumbrian prince, had in a time of peril hidden in the island of Iona, to where the great Irishman Columba had come from Ireland as a missionary. When Oswald returned to power he summoned to his kingdom Aidan, a high-minded Christian teacher, whom he made first bishop of Lindisfarne (Holy Island). Aidan being a Celt, had to do his work through interpreters, but he did it well, and laid the foundations of Christianity and learning in Northumbria. Cuthbert was another famous missionary. Rising from shepherd-boy to bishop, he impressed both king and peasant by the dignified simplicity and sincerity of his life. His place of meditation was a sea-girt rock by Lindisfarne, lonely and picturesque, and still called after his name. A curious fossil, with the mark of a cross, is plentiful there, and goes by the name of St Cuthbert's beads. Other famous teachers were Wilfrid of York, who founded the churches of Hexham and Ripon; Boisil, who founded Melrose, and Biscop, who founded Jarrow.

But perhaps the most celebrated of all was Bede, the "Venerable Bede," who lived at Jarrow and wrote forty-five learned books on all subjects, including music, astronomy, and medicine. All the scholars in England flocked to hear his teachings, and he was justly called "the father of English learning." He it was who first introduced into England the art of making glass.

His last work was to translate the Gospel of St John into Northumbrian English. This was in the year 735. Being too ill to hold a pen, he dictated to his favourite pupil. "Write quickly," he said, for he felt that he was dying. "It is finished," answered the lad, and the old man's heart was satisfied. In a faint, brave voice he chanted the *Gloria*, and so died singing.

In those days there was, of course, no such thing as printing. Every manuscript was written and rewritten, carefully, by hand, and treasured as a sacred possession in the seats of learning. So proud were they of their manuscripts that they beautified them with illustrations in colour. Many of these manuscripts have, of course, been destroyed; for instance, the Danes in 875 burnt the priceless library of Bishop Acca at Hexham, destroying in one day the treasured collection of a lifetime; but many remain to show the love of learning which existed even then. Bishop Edfrid, who lived in the little rocky island of Lindisfarne, made a copy of the Gospels, which is looked upon with wonder even to-day. Strings of beautiful birds and quaint animals are drawn upon his pages; evangelists with mantles of purple and tunics of blue, pink, or green. With the writing clear and beautiful, the decorations showing the greatest care and devotion, this manuscript of one thousand two hundred years ago has been the delight of thousands, and comes down to us to witness to the loving care of the scholars of old in the days before printing was known.

Great as was their love of beautiful manuscripts, they had an equally noble passion for grand buildings. A superb monument of simple dignity and religious grandeur is the Norman Cathedral at Durham, commenced by Bishop Carilef in 1093, and finished by Bishop Flambard in 1128. Occupying a wonderful position at the top of a wooded hill, around which flows the beautiful river Wear, Durham Cathedral is in itself one of the noblest buildings in the world. While the Church in those troublous times kept thus a storehouse of learning for serious scholars, other methods kept the people informed of the more stirring events of their day.

In the old days, when no newspapers existed to tell people the news, when books were scarce and history was not taught to every lad as a part of his training, the ballad-writer and the wandering minstrel played a very important part. Ballads, sometimes really fine pieces of poetry, sometimes a mere halting troop of lame lines, were made upon every occasion of local or general interest. They were sung to simple and often beautiful tunes or chants. The best of the minstrels were welcome to the halls of the nobles, and even to the king himself; the poorest of them sang on the village green. The ballads were learnt and repeated by the folk of the country-side; some were in later times printed on loose sheets, but at first they were handed on from mouth to mouth. Alterations and errors often crept in; mistakes due to a sameness of sound. For instance, in the old ballad of *Mary Ambree,* a soldier is referred to as "Sir John Major," probably meaning Sergeant-major. In one of the versions of the battle of Chevy Chase, Henry Percy was said to have been killed there, whereas he really lived on to be slain at Shrewsbury. But, despite such occasional blunders, the ballads on the whole throw a vivid light on the manners and customs of the old days, as well as being usually stirring and sometimes strikingly noble and pathetic pieces of poetry. They deal as a rule rather with the side currents than with the main stream of history; but they express themselves with such homely force and directness that they bring home to us with wonderful clearness the character of the vigorous manly men with whose doings they are chiefly concerned.

During the last one hundred and fifty years many able men have laboured to collect old ballads, writing them down from the mouths of the country-folk and printing them in books with notes of explanation. One of the earliest thus to collect ballads seriously was Bishop Percy; the best known is Sir Walter Scott, of whose interest in the subject Lockhart, his biographer, writes very pleasantly.

Prefaced to many of the stirring tales in this present book are lines from the old Border ballads from which they are taken. It is to be hoped that readers will be tempted sooner or later to read the rest of these fine ballads for themselves.

Chapter IV

Sir Patrick Spens

"The king sits in Dunfermline town
Drinking the blood-red wine;
'O where shall I get a well-skilled skipper
To sail this new ship of mine?'"

ALMOST every collection of Scottish songs contains this picturesque old ballad, which refers to a very remote time in Scottish history, probably the end of the thirteenth century. King Alexander III. of Scotland died in 1285; he had the bitter grief of seeing all his children die before him. His daughter Margaret had been married to Eric, King of Norway, and she left a daughter also called Margaret, and known as the "Maid of Norway." This maid was now heiress to the Scottish throne, and it is natural to suppose that the lonely king should wish her to return to Scotland, and should send a richly appointed ship to fetch her back. And although there is no strictly historical record of such an expedition, the truth of the ballad is made more probable by the fact that it opens in the fine old town of Dunfermline.

Dunfermline was a favourite residence of Alexander, who was killed in its neighbourhood by a fall from his horse, and was buried in the abbey there, the ruins of which beautiful structure still remain.

In this ballad the king is feasting at Dunfermline

town, and calls for a skilful mariner to sail his new ship. An old knight at the king's right hand answers that the best sailor who ever sailed the sea is Sir Patrick Spens. So the king writes a letter, sealing it with his own hand, and sends it to Sir Patrick, commanding him to sail away to Norway over the white sea-foam and bring home the maid.

Now every good sailor dreaded the rough Northern seas in winter, so though the brave Sir Patrick laughed aloud when he began to read, he wept blinding tears before he had ended. "Who has done this deed?" he cried; "who has told the king of me and urged him to send us out at this time of the year to sail on the stormy sea? Yet, wind, wet, hail, or sleet, we must set out, for 'tis we who must fetch home the maid."

So they set sail on a Monday morning, and reached Norway on a Wednesday. History tells us that Eric of Norway was very unwilling to part with his daughter. This probably accounts for the fact that the old ballad tells us that the Scotsmen had only been there a fortnight when the lords of Norway began to say that Sir Patrick and his men were spending the gold of their king and queen. "Ye lie," cried Sir Patrick, "loudly I hear ye lie, for I brought with me over the sea enough red gold and white money to supply the wants of my men. Make ready, make ready, my merry men; we will sail at daybreak." "Alack," quoth the men, "a deadly storm is brewing. Yesterday evening the new moon was seen carrying the old moon in her arms; we shall certainly come to harm if we go to sea."

Barely had they sailed three leagues when the sky darkened, the wind blew loudly, and the sea grew boisterous. Soon they were in the midst of a terrible storm. The anger of the sea was far more dreadful than the anger of the lords of Norway. The anchors broke away, the topmasts snapped, and the waves came over the broken ship, tearing her sides asunder. "O where shall I get a good sailor to take the helm while I climb the tall topmast to see if I can espy land?" "That I fear ye never will," cried a sailor as he took the helm, and scarcely had Sir Patrick gone a step when a plank started in the ship's side and the water came pouring in.

"Fetch a web of silken cloth, and fetch a web of twine," cried Sir Patrick, "and cast them down to our ship's side!" For it was the custom in those days, when a leak could not be reached from inside the vessel, to cast down some closely woven stuff in the hope that the suction of the water would drag it across the leak and stop thus the fatal inrush of water. Alas! all their efforts failed. Then the ballad-writer says somewhat grimly of the dandies among the Scottish lords that whereas at first they grumbled to see the water spoil their fine cork-heeled shoes, when the storm had done its fatal work the sea was "above their hats"!

"And many was the feather bed
That fluttered on the foam;
And many was the gude lord's son
That never mair came home!

The ladyes wrang their fingers white;
The maidens tore their hair,
A' for the sake of their true loves;
For them they'll see nae mair.

O lang, lang may the ladyes sit,
Wi' their fans into their hand,
Before they see Sir Patrick Spens
Come sailing to the strand!

And lang, lang may the maidens sit,
  With their goud kaims[1] in their hair,
A' waiting for their ain dear loves !
  For them they'll see nae mair.

O forty miles off Aberdeen,
  'Tis fifty fathoms deep,
And there lies gude Sir Patrick Spens,
  Wi' the Scots lords at his feet."

[1] Golden combs.

Chapter V

Auld Maitland

"'Wha holds this house?' young Edward cried,
'Or wha gives it o'er to me?'
''Tis I will keep my good old house,
While my house will keep me!'"

THE story of Auld Maitland is said to be taken from a very old ballad, and known chiefly to the people who lived in the neighbourhood of Ettrick Forest. The old folks there would while away the long winter evenings by singing of the deeds of their ancestors, and the ballad of *Auld Maitland*, as thus chanted, was written down by the mother of James Hogg, the "Ettrick Shepherd."

The castle of Thirlestane stood on the river Leader, and still, in its restored form, deserves its name of "the darksome house." It may have often withstood the English during the Baliol wars, and hatred of the English and of Edward I. is expressed with extreme virulence throughout the poem. Here is the story:—

There lived in the south country a king named Edward, who wore the crown unworthily for fifty years. This king had a nephew, strong in blood and bone, who bore the same hateful name. One day the young man came before the king, and kneeling low, he said, "A boon, a boon I crave of thee, my good uncle. Oft have I wished to take part in our long wars in fair Scotland. Grant me fifteen hundred chosen strong men to ride there with me."

"Certainly thou shalt have them, and more, and I myself, though old and grey, will see thy host arrayed for battle."

King Edward sent hither and thither, and assembled fifteen hundred men on Tyne side, and three times as many at North Berwick, all bound for battle. They marched up the banks of Tweed, burning the Merse and Teviotdale, and up and down the Lammermoor Hills, until they came to the darksome house called, by some, "Leader-Town."

"Who holds this house?" cried young Edward, "or who gives it over to me?" He was answered, as proudly, by a grey-haired knight: "I hold my house of Scotland's king, who pays me in meat and fee, and I will hold it as long as it will stand together."

Thereupon the English brought up their sows[1] to the wall with many a heavy sound, but the soldiers on the wall cast down blazing pitch and tar barrels, to consume the formidable machine. They also threw down stones and beams and darts from their springalds,[2] and slew many of the English.

Fifteen days they besieged the castle of Auld Maitland, but left him at the end of that time unhurt within his stone stronghold.

They loaded fifteen ships with as much spoil as they could carry away from the district around, and claimed that now they had conquered Scotland with buckler, bow, and brand. So they sailed away to France to meet the old

[1] A military engine framed of wood, covered with hides and mounted on wheels, so that, being rolled forward to the foot of the wall, it served as a shed to defend the miners underneath it and their battering-rams from the stones and arrows of the soldiers above.

[2] Large crossbows worked by machinery.

The Siege of Maitland Castle

King Edward, who was burning every castle, tower, and town that he met with. They came at last to the town of Billop-Grace, where Auld Maitland's three sons were at school.

Edward had quartered the arms of Scotland with his own. "See'st thou what I see?" said the eldest son to the youngest; "if that be true that yonder standard says, then are we all three fatherless, and Scotland conquered up and down. Never will we bow to the conquerer. Let us go, my two brothers, and try our chance in an adventure?" Thereupon they saddled two black horses and a grey, and rode before day-dawn to King Edward's army. Arrived there, they hovered round, and Maitland begged to be allowed to carry the king's standard, the Golden Dragon.

"Where wast thou born and bred, and in what country?" demanded the knight who bore the banner. "I was born in the north of England," answered Maitland; "my father was a knight and my mother a lady, and I myself am a squire of high renown, and may well carry the banner of a king." "Never had the son of an Englishmen such an eye or brow," answered the knight; "thou art more like Auld Maitland than any man I have ever seen; yet God grant that such a gloomy brow I never see again; he slew and wounded many of our men."

At the mention of his father's name Maitland's anger burst out, and lifting up a gilded dagger that hung low by his knee, he struck fiercely at the standard-bearer, and, catching hold of the corner of the standard, rode swiftly away with it, crying to his brothers, "Is it not time to flee?" "Ay, by my sooth," they both shouted, "we will bear you company." So they rode off at hot speed, the pursuers following. The youngest Maitland, turning round in the path, drew his brand and killed fifteen of the foremost, and the rest fell back. Then he dug his spurs into the sides of his faithful grey, until both the sides ran blood. "Thou must carry me away, or my life lies in pledge," he cried.

About daybreak the brothers arrived at their uncle's castle, who, seeing the three Scottish lads with pursuers riding hard at their heels, ordered the portcullis to be drawn up and the drawbridge let down, for that they should lodge with him that night in spite of all England.

When the three came inside the gate, they leapt down from their horses, and taking three long spears in their hands, they fought till it was full daylight, killing and wounding many of the Englishmen round the drawbridge. Some of the dead were carted away in waggons, and stones were heaped upon the rest as they lay in the gutter.

King Edward proclaimed at his pavilion door that three lads of France, disguised, and with false words, had come and stolen away the standard, and had slain his men in their lawful attempt to regain it.

"It ill befits a crowned king to lie," said the youngest Maitland, "and he shall be reproved for it before I taste meat or drink."

Straightway he went before King Edward, and, kneeling low, begged leave to speak a word with him. "Man, thou shalt have leave to speak, even though thou shouldst speak all day," answered the king.

"Ye said," spoke the youngest Maitland, "that three young lads of France had stolen away the standard with a false tale, and slain many men. But we are not lads of France, and never have pretended to be; we are three lads of fair Scotland, and the sons of Auld Maitland, nor are there men in all your host dare fight us three to three."

"Now, by my sooth," said the young Edward, who stood by, "Ye shall be well fitted, for Percy shall fight with the eldest, and Egbert Lunn with thee, and William of Lancaster with the other, and the surviving brother shall fight with me. Remember, Percy, how oft the Scot has cowered before thee; I will give thee a rig of land for every drop of Maitland blood."

So they set to, and the eldest Maitland clanked Percy over the head and wounded him so deeply that the best blood of his body ran down his hair. "I have slain one," shouted Maitland to his brothers; "slay ye the other two, and that will be good company, and if the two shall slay ye both, ye shall get no help from me."[1]

But Egbert Lunn was like a baited bear and had seen many battles, and when Maitland saw that his youngest brother was having the worst of it, he could not restrain himself longer, and shouting, "I am no king; my word shall not stand," he struck Egbert over the head and slew him. "Now I have slain two; slay ye one for good company," he cried; "neither shall ye get any help from me even if the one shall slay ye both." So the two brothers slew the third, and hung him over the drawbridge for all the host to see.

Then they rode and ran, but still got not away, but hovered round, boasting: "We be three lads of fair Scotland that fain would see some fighting."

When young Edward heard this, he cried wrathfully, "I'll take yon lad and bind him, and bring him bound to thee."

"Now God forbid that ever thou shouldst try that,"

[1] According to the laws of chivalry, having slain his own man, he could, if he pleased, come to the assistance of the others.

said the king; "we have lost three worthy leaders; wouldst thou be the fourth? Never again would I be happy if thou wert to hang on yonder drawbridge."

But Edward struck fiercely at Maitland, cleaving his stout helmet and biting right near his brain. When Maitland saw his own blood flowing he threw away his weapon, and springing angrily at young Edward's throat, he swung him thrice about and flung him on the ground, holding him there though he was of great strength.

"Now let him up," cried King Edward, "let him come to me, and for thy deed thou shalt have three earldoms."

"Nay," replied Maitland, "never shall it be said in France or in Scotland that Edward once lay under me and got up again," and with that he pierced him through the heart and hung him over the drawbridge with the other three.

"Now take from me my bed of feathers," said the king, "make me a bed of straw. Would that I had not lived to see the day that makes my heart so sad."

Chapter VI

The Mystery of the Eildons

"Before their eyes the Wizard lay
As if he had not been dead a day.
His hoary beard in silver roll'd,
He seemed some seventy winters old.
High and majestic was his look,
At which the fellest friends had shook,
And all unruffled was his face;
They trusted his soul had gotten grace."

SCOTT: *Lay of the Last Minstrel.*

JUST above Melrose, the ruined abbey of which is one of the beauties of Scotland, there rises a striking mass of three hills known as "the triple Eildons." They rise very high above the surrounding land, and are steep enough to need a very hard scramble to mount to the very summit; but once at the top the view is wonderful indeed. On a fine day the Tweed can be seen winding in and out most picturesquely, till it loses itself in the low distant haze of the North Sea, thirty miles away. But even grander is the view of the entire line of the Cheviots, like a huge wall, fifty miles long, seen to immense advantage from Eildon, which towers over the rich valleys of Tweed and Teviot that lie between. One of the legends of the triple Eildons is that King Arthur lies sleeping beneath them, some day to awaken. Tradition says that he fought a great battle near here, by Gala Water, in the Vale of Woe.

However that may be, it is certain that at the foot of Eildon lie many famous dead. In Melrose Abbey lies the heart of Robert Bruce, and also the body of the strong King Alexander II., he who first subdued and made obedient the wild tribes of Argyle. Here, too, is buried the brave Douglas who died so gallantly on the field of Otterbourne; and also of another brave Douglas who got his death wound at Poictiers.

Sir Walter Scott, who did more than any other man to spread all over the world the knowledge of Scotland, Scottish history, Scottish romance, and Scottish character, lies buried on the southern side of Eildon, in the rival abbey of Dryburgh. But Melrose can claim a man who in his day was an object of the deepest wonder and terror—Michael Scott, the famous wizard of the thirteenth century, he who brought the learning of Aristotle to expound to Western Europe, he whom Dante described as learned in every deep spell of the magic arts. Perhaps he was only a scientist, born before his time; yet even to-day old folk in the country remember that it was he who is said to have cleft the head of Eildon Hill into three!

One of the many strange tales told of Michael Scott is this:—

They say that the lord of Morpeth, in Northumberland, promised the great wizard a rich reward if he would only make the sea roll up the valley of the pretty river Wansbeck till it reached Morpeth, so that vessels could sail up to the town. The distance is seven miles, and the wizard, declaring the matter a most simple one, prepared his magic spell. He then said that if a certain man would run from the sea to the town, and on no account look back, whatever he heard, the desire of the lord would be satisfied. The man no sooner started to run than he heard the waters following him. Faster and faster he went, and faster and faster came the ocean, dashing and roaring, never overtaking him, but always so near his heels as to fill him with ever greater and greater terror.

Before he had finished the third mile he was in such a state of alarm that he could not resist the impulse to see what was happening. He turned round, and the spell was broken; the waters had followed him thus far, but would come no further. Even the best of wizards will fail when his instructions are not obeyed.

So says the story. People are free to believe it or not, as they please. It is certain that the sea runs nearly three miles up the Wansbeck valley, and there stops; but many people think that that is explained by the natural rise of the land!

The story of how Michael Scott came to divide the Eildon Hill into three runs as follows:—

The wizard had one very active little demon, who was always bothering his master to give him something to do. First Michael commanded him to put a barrier across the Tweed at Kelso, thinking to keep him quiet for at least a week; it was done in a single night, and again the demon demanded work. Then Michael set him to divide Eildon into three; this also was done in a night, and again the demon came clamouring for employment. So in despair the wizard ordered him to make ropes out of sea-sand! This, of course, is impossible, as the sand will not hold together. But if you go down to the shore on the south-east coast of Scotland on a dark and stormy night, you can still hear what sounds like the demon moaning and groaning over his impossible task; and there is certainly a barrier across the Tweed at Kelso, and the Eildon Hill is certainly divided into three! So you may believe as much as you please of this story.

Another tale that is told of the magic powers of this famous man relates that he was once chosen to go as ambassador from the King of Scotland to the King of France on urgent business. Instead of going, as is usual in such cases, with a number of followers, he conjured up a demon shaped like a huge black horse, and rode away over the sea. When half-way across the North Sea the horse said to his rider:—

"What do the old women of Scotland say at bed-time?" Had the magician fallen into the trap and named a prayer, the demon would have disappeared and the wizard would have been drowned! But Michael Scott merely commanded his steed to go on quickly and not to talk. Very soon he came to Paris, tied his horse to the gate of the French king's palace, and boldly entered and stated his business. The French king sneered at an ambassador who was not followed by a train of knights, and began at once to refuse all he asked. "Wait a moment, your Majesty," said Michael, "till you have seen my horse stamp three times."

At the first stamp the ground so shook that every steeple in Paris rocked, making all the bells ring loudly; at the second stamp the king heard behind him a loud crash that made him leap three feet in the air; looking round, he saw that three of the towers of his palace had fallen; the horse raised his foot to stamp a third time, but the king was so terrified that he shouted hastily that he would grant all that Michael asked if only he would keep his horse from stamping!

Whether this tale is true or not, Michael Scott was certainly one of the ambassadors sent to bring back the Maid of Norway to Scotland on the death of King

Alexander III. He wrote many learned books, and possessed many others; and they say that when he was buried at Melrose many of these same magic books were buried with him.

To this romantic district of the Eildons belonged True Thomas, Thomas the Rhymer, or Thomas of Ercildoune, as he was variously called, who was held in awe by Border-folks as a prophet. The ruins of his tower are still shown by the pretty river Leader, just about two miles above the spot where it joins the Tweed. The Rhymer seems to have died a few years before 1300; but despite the passing of six centuries he is still remembered. The story of how he gained his prophetic powers is quite worth hearing, whether we believe it or not.

The tale goes that Thomas was on Huntlie bank, near the Eildon Hills, when he saw a wonderful lady approaching him. She was dressed in grass-green silk, with a mantle of fine velvet, and the noble horse on which she rode had silver bells in its mane. Thomas was so surprised at this remarkable sight that when the lady came near he dropped on his knee and pulled off his cap, and cried out, reverently, that she must be the Queen of Heaven. But she answered that she was Queen of fair Elfland, and dared him, with a witching glance, to kiss her lips. The bold and gallant Thomas did not need a second invitation, and promptly kissed the fairy, when she seized upon him and fled away with him swifter than the wind.

Soon all living land was left behind, and they came to a wild place where three roads met. One was a narrow path, beset with thorns and briers; and this the fairy said was the road of righteousness, which very few people ever troubled to find. Another was a broad and attractive road, which was the way of sinners; whilst the third, a pretty winding road, led to Elfland, and thither they went together.

Soon there was neither sun nor moon to lighten the way, and Thomas and his companion waded through rivers above the knee. The sea moaned and roared in the dread darkness, and Thomas somehow found that they waded oft through streams of red blood—blood that had been shed on earth. Then they came to a beautiful garden, and the Elfland queen gave Thomas an apple to eat, saying:—

"Take this for thy wages, true Thomas; it will give thee the tongue that can never lie." Poor Thomas turned pale at the thought of such a gift. "Let my tongue be my own!" he pleaded; "how shall I buy or sell in any market, flatter a prince, or compliment a lady, if you give me such a tongue!"

But the Elfland queen would take no denial, and Thomas had to do her behest, wherefore for the rest of his life Thomas carried with him this gift of truthfulness.

Chapter VII

Black Agnes of Dunbar

THE fortress of Dunbar was always a very important one to the Scots. It commanded the coast road from England across the Border to Edinburgh, not only one of the best routes in itself, but one which had the additional advantage to the English that by following it they could keep in touch with their ships. So it is not surprising that many stirring events in history took place at this historic town.

King Edward I. of England won a very important victory at Dunbar during his first invasion of Scotland, and to the place which had witnessed the triumph of the father, his son, Edward II., fled for safety after his defeat at Bannockburn, taking ship thence back to England. In the time of Mary Queen of Scots the fortress was held by Earl Bothwell; from here he consented to the surrender of poor Mary, and here he rested in safety before his final flight to Scandinavia. Oliver Cromwell fought and won at Dunbar his desperate battle with the Scottish Presbyterians, the fate of which for some time hung in the balance. Cromwell considered the place so valuable that he had new harbour works made there, and a portion of his work, forming part of the east pier of the present much larger harbour, is still to be seen.

The last time that Dunbar resounded to the march of an army bent on immediate fight was in 1745, when the boastful English general, Sir John Cope, landed here to engage the Highland followers of Prince Charles Edward (called the "Young Pretender"). Prince Charlie was at Edinburgh, and Dunbar Castle commanded the road into England. Cope asserted that the Highlanders would run away at the mere sight of his army. He marched westward, but was surprised in the early morning by his enemies when near Prestonpans. In less than ten minutes it was the unprepared English who were flying in disorder, utterly routed.

The foregoing is but a brief outline of the stormy history of those grey and ruined battlements overlooking the bleak North Sea at the southernmost point of entrance to the noble Firth of Forth. The mention of these stirring incidents, however, will serve to show what a very important place Dunbar was, and that it was necessary to Scottish safety that a strong hand should have charge of its fortress. We are now to see how at one of the most critical hours a woman was to hold command, and to hold it worthily.

Early in the reign of King Edward III. of England Scottish affairs were in some confusion. King Robert Bruce had lately died, leaving a son, King David II., then only five years old. That great leader and friend of Bruce, Randolph, Earl of Moray, was appointed Guardian of Scotland, but he too soon died. Edward III., anxious to interfere in Scottish affairs, agreed to help Edward Balliol to make himself king of the Scots. So an English army was again in Scotland, and one of the places they were keenest to take was the fortress of Dunbar.

The castle was a very strong one. It was built on a

Black Agnes

chain of great rocks that stretched out to sea, and could only be reached from land by one road, which was, of course, strictly guarded. The lord of the castle was the Earl of March (the word March in those days meant a border-land), but he was away with the Scottish army, and his wife was in charge of the castle. She was the daughter of that brave Earl of Moray, Guardian of Scotland, who has just been mentioned. The English army was led by an experienced general, the Earl of Salisbury, and he probably thought that he would not have much trouble in overcoming "Black Agnes," as the dark-haired countess was called.

He soon discovered that she was of heroic mould, however, for though he himself led the storming-parties, she on her side, urging on her men in person, hurled back his every attack. The Lady Agnes was quite fearless, and treated the siege as if it were a pastime to be enjoyed. When the English, with machines made for the purpose, hurled heavy stones against the walls, Black Agnes would call one of her maidens with a napkin to wipe off the dust that they made! The biggest of all the English war-machines was called a *sow,* and when it was brought to the walls the countess cried out in rough jest that it was surrounded by little pigs. At the same moment a mass of rock, which she had caused to be loosened, was hurled by her men on to the English, crushing their *sow* and many soldiers with it.

At last there seemed a chance for the English. Near midnight a Scot came into their camp, saying that he was ready to betray the castle for a reward. The Earl of Salisbury and some chosen knights rode carefully forward, and found the gate open and the portcullis raised, as the man had promised. But for all that, they doubted if Black Agnes could so far relax her vigilance;

wherefore instead of the earl entering first, he sent forward a retainer. His caution was soon justified, for no sooner had this man passed the gate than the portcullis fell. It was a trick to capture the earl, but the Scots were disappointed this time.

The gallant English lord was loud in admiration of the brave Scottish lady who was thus defying him. Once when examining the defences with a lieutenant, an arrow struck his companion dead. "The countess's love-arrows pierce to the heart," said Salisbury, on his return to the camp. Despite the courtly manner in which the well-bred baron referred to the lady, however, he did not relax his efforts to overcome her.

Salisbury's land forces had now surrounded the castle on the land side, while his ships at sea completed the blockade. The garrison was threatened with starvation. Greater and greater became the privations of the heroic defenders. The countess, no less brave than ever, hoped on, though ground for hope grew less and less. She could not bring herself to think of defeat, and her brave, bright face still gave courage and inspiration to all.

Meantime the story of the struggle and difficulties of the defenders was raising up helpers, and Sir Alexander Ramsay of Dalhousie got ready a light vessel filled with provisions and manned by forty brave Scots, who only waited for a dark night to make the attempt to steal past the English fleet. They lay hidden by the Bass Rock, a lofty islet at the mouth of the Firth of Forth, some seven or eight miles from Dunbar, until one starless night they stole very cautiously down the wild coast-line of Haddingtonshire, sometimes all but bumping into an English vessel in the dark. Fortune favours the brave, and despite dangers and difficulties they got safely at last to the castle, whose distant light had been their guide. Be sure Black Agnes welcomed them! This proved to be the turning-point of the long siege. With fresh hope, the garrison made a sudden sally on the English, driving back their advance guard, and after five months of fierce but fruitless attempts, Salisbury was compelled to withdraw his forces and admit defeat. Nevertheless, the English were gallant enough to sing their praises of this Scottish heroine; their minstrels made songs in her honour, in one of which Salisbury is made to say:—

"Came I early, came I late,
I found Black Agnes at the gate."

Chapter VIII

The Young Tamlane

"He's ta'en her by the milk-white hand,
Among the leaves so green."

THIS tale belongs to the romantic side of the Border minstrelsy, and illustrates some of the common superstitions of olden times concerning elves and fairies. The scene is laid in the Selkirk or Ettrick Forest, a mountainous tract covered with the remains of the old Caledonian Forest. About a mile above Selkirk is a plain called Carterhaugh, and here may still be seen those fairy rings of which it was believed that anyone sleeping upon one will wake in a fairy city. And here was, and perhaps still is, an ancient well. The ballad opens by telling how all young maids were forbidden to come or go by way of Carterhaugh, "for young Tamlane (or Thomalin) is there," and every one going by Carterhaugh is obliged to leave him something in pledge. But the Lady Janet, the fairest of the Selkirk lasses, was obstinate, and declared that she would come or go to Carterhaugh, as she pleased, "and ask no leave of him," since the land there belonged to her by hereditary right. She kilted her green mantle above her knee, and braided her yellow hair above her brow, and off she went to Carterhaugh. When she got to the well, she found the steed of the elfin knight Tamlane standing there, but he himself was away.

"She hadna pu'd a red, red rose,
A rose but barely three;
Till up and starts a wee, wee man
At Lady Janet's knee.

Says—'Why pu' ye the rose, Janet?
What gars (makes) ye break the tree?
Or why come ye to Carterhaugh,
Withouten leave of me?'

Says—'Carterhaugh it is mine ain;
My daddy gave it me:
I'll come and gang to Carterhaugh,
And ask nae leave o' thee.'"

But Tamlane took her by the hand and worked upon her his spells, which no maiden might resist, however proud she might be.

When she came back to her father's hall, she looked pale and wan; and it seemed that she had some sore sickness. She ceased to take any pleasure in combing her yellow hair, and everything she ate seemed like to be her death. When her ladies played at ball, she, once the strongest player, was now the faintest. One day her father spoke out, and said he, "Full well I know that you must have some lover." She said:—

"'It my love were an earthly knight,
As he's an elfin grey,
I wouldna give my own true love
For no lord that ye hae.'"

Then she prinked herself, and preened herself, all by the light of the moon alone, and went away to Carterhaugh, to speak with Tamlane. When she got to the well, she found the steed standing, but Tamlane was away. She had barely pulled a double rose, when up started the elf.

"Why pull ye the rose, Janet?" says he; "why pull ye the rose within this garden green?" "The truth ye'll tell me, Tamlane; were ye ever in holy chapel, or received into the Christian Church?" "The truth I'll tell thee, Janet; a knight was my father, and a lady was my mother, like your own parents. Randolph, Earl Moray, was my sire; Dunbar, Earl March, is thine. We loved when we were children, which yet you may remember. When I was a boy just turned nine, my uncle sent for me to hunt, and hawk, and ride with him, and keep him company. There came a wind out of the north, a deep sleep came over me, and I fell from my horse. The queen of the fairies took me off to yon green hill, and now I'm a fairy, lithe and limber. In Fairyland we know neither sickness nor pain. We quit our body, or repair unto them, when we please. We can inhabit, earth, or air, as we will. Our shapes and size we can convert to either large or small. We sleep in rose-buds, revel in the stream, wanton lightly on the wind, or glide on a sunbeam. I would never tire, Janet, to dwell in Elfland, were it not that every seven years a tithe is paid to hell, and I am so fair of flesh, I fear 'twill be myself. If you dare to win your true love, you have no time to lose. To-night is Hallowe'en, and the fairy folk ride. If you would win your true love, bide at Miles Cross." Miles Cross is about half a mile from Carterhaugh, and Janet asked how she should know Tamlane among so many unearthly knights. "The first company that passes by, let them go. The next company that passes by, let them go. The third company that passes by, I'll be one of those. First let pass the black steed, Janet, then let pass the brown; but grip the milk-white steed, and pull down the rider—

"For I ride on the milk-white steed,
And aye nearest the town;
Because I was a christened knight,
They gave me that renown."

Tamlane went on to explain that his fairy comrades would make every effort to disgust her with her captive. They would turn him in her very arms into an adder; they would change him into a burning faggot, into a red-hot iron goad, but she must hold him fast. In order to remove the enchantment, she must dip him in a churn of milk, and then in a barrel of water. She must still persevere, for they would shape him in her arms into a badger, eel, dove, swan, and, last of all, into a naked man, but

"Cast your green mantle over me,
I'll be myself again."

So fair Janet in her green mantle went that gloomy night to Miles Cross. The heavens were black, the place was inexpressibly dreary, a north wind raged; but there she stood, eagerly wishing to embrace her lover. Between the hours of twelve and one she heard strange eldrich sounds and the ringing of elfin bridles, which gladdened her heart. The oaten pipes of the fairies grew shrill, the hemlock blew clear. The fairies cannot bear solemn sounds or sober thoughts; they sing like skylarks, inspired by love and joy. Fair Janet stood upon the dreary heath, and the sounds waxed louder as the fairy train came riding on. Will o' the Wisp shone out as a twinkling light before them, and soon she saw the fairy bands passing. She let the black steed go by, and then the brown. But she gripped fast the milk-white steed, and pulled down the rider. Then up rose an eldrich cry, "He's won among us all!" As Janet grasped him in her arms the fairies changed him into a newt, an adder, and many other fantastic and terrifying shapes. She held him fast in every shape. They turned him at last into a naked man in her arms, but she wrapped him in her green mantle. At last her stedfast courage was rewarded, she redeemed the fairies' captive, and by so doing won his true love! Then up spoke the Queen of Fairies, "She that has borrowed young Tamlane has got a stately groom! She's taken the bonniest knight in all my company! But had I known, Tamlane," said the fairy queen, "had I known that a lady would borrow thee, I would have taken out thy two grey eyes, and put in wooden eyes. I would have taken out thy heart of flesh, Tamlane, and put in a heart of stone. I would have paid my tithe seven times to hell ere I would have let her win you away."

Chapter IX

The Gay Goss-Hawk

IN the opening lines of this old ballad Lord William is talking to the goss-hawk, who tells his master that he is looking pale and thin, and seeks to know the cause.

"O waly, waly, my gay goss-hawk,
Gin your feathering be sheen!"
"And waly, waly, my master dear,
Gin ye look pale and lean!

O have ye tint [1] at tournament
Your sword, or yet your spear?
Or mourn ye for the Southern lass,
Whom ye may not win near?"

"I have not tint at tournament
My sword, nor yet my spear;
But sair [2] I mourn for my true love,
Wi' mony a bitter tear.

But weel's me on ye, my gay goss-hawk,
Ye can baith speak and flee;
Ye sall carry a letter to my love,
Bring an answer back to me."

[1] lost. [2] sore.

"But how sall I your true love find,
Or how suld I her know?
I bear a tongue ne'er wi' her spake,
An eye that ne'er her saw."

"O weel sall ye my true love ken,
Sae sune [1] as ye her see;
For, of a' the flowers of fair England,
The fairest flower is she.

The red that's on my true love's cheek
Is like blood-drops on the snaw;
The white that is on her breast bare,
Like the down o' the white sea-maw.

And even at my love's bour-door
There grows a flowering birk; [2]
And ye maun sit and sing thereon
As she gangs to the kirk.

And four-and-twenty fair ladyes
Will to the Mass repair;
But weel may ye my ladye ken,
The fairest ladye there."

Lord William has written a love-letter,
Put it under his pinion grey;
An' he is awa' to Southern land
As fast as wings can gae.

And even at the ladye's bour [3]
There grew a flowering birk;
And he sat down and sung thereon
As she gaed to the kirk.

[1] soon. [2] birch. [3] bower.

And weel he kent that ladye fair
  Amang her maidens free,
For the flower that springs in May morning
  Was not sae sweet as she.

He lighted at the ladye's yate [1]
  And sat him on a pin,[2]
And sang fu' sweet the notes o' love,
  Till a' was cosh [3] within.

And first he sang a low low note,
  And syne [4] he sang a clear;
And aye the o'erword [5] o' the sang
  Was—"Your love can no win here."

"Feast on, feast on, my maidens a',
  The wine flows you amang,
While I gang to my shot-window
  And hear yon bonnie bird's sang.

Sing on, sing on, my bonny bird,
  The sang ye sung yestreen,
For weel I ken, by your sweet singing
  Ye are frae my true love sen." [6]

O first he sang a merry song,
  And syne he sang a grave;
And syne he picked his feathers grey,
  To her the letter gave.

"Have there a letter from Lord William;
  He says he's sent ye three;

[1] gate. [2] pine. [3] quiet.
[4] then. [5] refrain [6] sent.

He canna wait your love langer,
But for your sake he'll die."

"Gae bid him bake his bridal bread,
And brew his bridal ale;
And I shall meet him in Mary's Kirk,
Lang, lang ere it be stale."

The lady's gane to her chamber,
And a moanfu' woman was she;
As gin [1] she had taken a sudden brash [2]
And were about to die.

"A boon, a boon, my father dear,
A boon I beg of thee!"
"Ask not that haughty Scottish lord,
For him ye ne'er shall see.

But for your honest asking else,
Weel granted it shall be."
"Then, gin I die in Southern land,
In Scotland gar [3] bury me.

And the first kirk that ye come to,
Ye's gar the mass be sung;
And the next kirk that ye come to
Ye's gar the bells be rung.

And when ye come to St Mary's Kirk,
Ye's tarry there till night."
And so her father pledged his word,
And so his promise plight.

[1] if. [2] illness. [3] cause.

She has ta'en her to her bigly bower
  As fast as she could fare;
And she has drank a sleepy draught,
  That she had mixed wi' care.

And pale, pale grew her rosy cheek,
  That was sae bright of blee,[1]
And she seemed to be as surely dead
  As any one could be.

Then spake her cruel step-minnie,[2]
  " Tak ye the burning lead,
And drap a drap on her bosome,
  To try if she be dead."

They took a drap o' boiling lead,
  They drapped it on her breast;
" Alas! alas!" her father cried,
  " She's dead without the priest."

She neither chattered with her teeth,
  Nor shivered with her chin;
" Alas! alas!" her father cried,
  " There is nae breath within."

Then up arose her seven brethren,
  And hewed to her a bier;
They hewed it frae the solid aik,[3]
  Laid it o'er wi' silver clear.

Then up and gat her seven sisters,
  And sewed to her a kell,[4]

[1] bloom. [2] mother. [3] oak. [4] shroud.

And every steek [1] that they put in
Sewed to a siller bell.

The first Scots kirk that they cam to,
They garred the bells be rung;
The next Scots kirk that they cam to,
They garred the mass be sung.

But when they cam to St Mary's Kirk,
There stude spearmen all on a row;
And up and started Lord William,
The chieftaine amang them a'.

"Set down, set down the bier," he said,
"Let me look her upon;"
But as soon as Lord William touched her hand,
Her colour began to come.

She brightened like the lily flower,
Till her pale colour was gone;
With rosy cheek, and ruby lip,
She smiled her love upon.

"A morsel of your bread, my lord,
And one glass of your wine;
For I have fasted these three lang days,
All for your sake and mine.

Gae hame, gae hame, my seven bauld brothers,
Gae hame and blaw your horn!
I trow [2] ye wad hae gi'en me the skaith,[3]
But I've gi'en you the scorn.

[1] stitch. [2] reckon. [3] harm.

Commend me to my grey father,
  That wished my soul gude rest;
But wae be to my cruel step-dame,
  Garred burn me on the breast."

" Ah! woe to you, you light woman!
  And ill death may ye die!
For we left father and sisters at hame,
  Breaking their hearts for thee."

Chapter X

The Corbies

TWO ancient songs have come down to us in which the principal speakers are supposed to be Corbies, carrion-crows or ravens, birds which feed on the flesh of the dead. In both songs the birds discuss a dead knight upon whose rich body they wish to feed. But deep interest lies in the fact that the two song-writers present entirely different views of the case. One appeals to our feelings with a beautiful and touching picture of devotion, the knight's companions proving true to him in death. The other is far more grim, and causes us to shudder at the utter loneliness of the dead man, deserted by all those who in life were beholden to his friendship. Both are powerful and striking examples of ancient vigour and directness.

THE TWA CORBIES

As I was walking all alane,
I heard twa corbies making a mane ; [1]
The tane unto the t'other say,
" Where sall we gang and dine to-day ? "—

" In behint yon auld fail dyke,
I wot there lies a new-slain knight ;

[1] moan.

The Twa Corbies

And naebody kens that he lies there,
But his hawk, his hound, and lady fair.

His hound is to the hunting gane,
His hawk, to fetch the wild-fowl hame,
His lady's ta'en another mate,
Sa we may mak our dinner sweet.

Ye'll sit on his white hause-bane,[1]
And I'll pick out his bonny blue een :
Wi' ae lock o' his gowden hair,
We'll theek[2] our nest when it grows bare.[3]

Mony a one for him makes mane,
But nane sall ken where he is gane ;
O'er his white banes, when they are bare,
The wind sall blaw for evermair."

THE THREE RAVENS

There were three ravens sat on a tre,
They were as black as they might be :

The one of them said to his mate,
" Where shall we our breakfast take? "—

" Downe in yonder greenë field,
There lies a knight slain under his shield ;

[1] neck. [2] thatch.
[3] Variant reading—
" We'll theek our nest—it's a' blawn bare."

" His hounds they lie downe at his feete,
So well they their master keepe;

" His hawkes they flie so eagerlie,
There's no fowle dare come him nie.

" Down there comes a fallow doe,
As great with yong as she might goe.

" She lift up his bloudy hed,
And kist his wounds that were so red.

" She got him up upon her backe,
And carried him to earthen lake.

" She buried him before the prime,
She was dead her selfe ere even song time.

" God send every gentleman,
Such hawkes, such houndes, and such a leman."

Chapter XI

Otterbourne and Chevy Chase

"It fell about the Lammas-tide,
When moor-men win their hay,
The doughty Douglas bound him to ride
Into England, to drive a prey."

THE ballads of *Otterbourne* and *Chevy Chase* record the Scottish and English versions of a most stubborn Border battle. Whichever of the two contains the greater amount of truth, it is clear that the day was a bloody one, and that, moreover, it was fought on both sides with a chivalrous admiration for the powers of the other which is characteristic of those strife-loving days. Sir Philip Sidney wrote of it: "I never heard the old song of Percy and Douglas, that I found not my heart moved more than with a trumpet."

The ballad of *Chevy Chase* is of later date than its rival, and it contains certainly one misstatement of historical fact, since Hotspur outlived the fight at Chevy Chase (1388) and was slain some fifteen years later at the battle of Shrewsbury (1403).

The Scottish version of the battle of Otterbourne tells us that it was about the Lammas-tide or haymaking time of the year 1388 when the brave Earl of Douglas, with his brother, the Earl of Murray, made a foray into England, with a gay band of Gordons, Graemes, and Lindsays. He burned Tynedale and half of Bamborough and Otterdale, and marching up to Newcastle, rode round about the castle, crying, "Who is lord of this castle, and who is its lady?"

Then up spake proud Lord Percy, known as *Hotspur*, and said, "I am the lord of this castle, and my wife is the gay lady of it."

"That pleases me well," answered Douglas, "yet, ere I cross the Border hills, one of us shall die."

Then Percy took his long spear, shod with metal, and rode right furiously at the Douglas; but his lady, looking from the castle wall, grew pale as she saw her proud lord go down before the Scottish spear.

"Had we two been alone, with never an eye to see, I would have slain thee, but thy lance I will carry with me," said Douglas, and, to complete the disgrace, this lance bore attached to it the Percy pennon.

"Go then to Otterbourne," said Percy, "and wait there for me, and if I come not before the end of three days, call me a false knight."

"Otterbourne is a pleasant and a bonny place," answered Douglas; "but though the deer run wild among the hills and dales, and the birds fly wild from tree to tree, yet is there neither bread nor kale nor aught else to feed me and my men. Yet will I wait thee at Otterbourne to give thee welcome, and if thou come not in three days' time, false lord, will I call thee!"

"By the might of Our Lady, I will come," cried the proud Percy. "And I," answered Douglas, "plight thee my troth that I will meet thee there."

So Douglas and his men encamped at Otterbourne, and sent out their horses to pasture.

But before the peep of dawn, up spake a little page: "Waken ye, waken ye, my good lord; the Percy is upon us!" "Ye lie, ye lie," shouted Douglas; "yesterday,

Percy had not men enough to fight us. But if thou lie not, the finest bower in Otterbourne shall be thy reward, and if what thou sayest prove false, thou shalt be hanged on the highest tree in Otterbourne. Yet I have dreamed a dreary dream; I dreamed that a dead man won a battle and that I was that dead man."

So Douglas belted on his good broadsword, and ran to the field, but forgot his helmet, and Percy and the Douglas fought with their swords together till the blood ran down like rain, and the Douglas fell, wounded on the brow.

Then he called to him his little foot-page and told him to run quickly and bring to him his sister's son, Sir Hugh Montgomery.

"My good nephew," said Douglas, "the death of one matters not; last night I dreamed a dreary dream, but yet I know the day is thine. My wound is deep; take thou the vanguard; bury me in the bracken high that grows on yonder lea, and let no man living know that a Scot lies there. And know that I am glad to die in battle, like my good forefathers, and not on a bed of sickness."

Montgomery lifted up his noble lord, while his eyes wept salt tears, and hid him in the bracken bush that his followers might not see, and before daylight the Scots slew many a gallant Englishman. The good Gordons steeped hose and shoes in the blood of the English; the Lindsays flew about like fire till the battle was ended, and Percy and Montgomery fought till the blood ran down between them.

"Now, yield thee, yield thee, Percy," cried Sir Hugh, "or I vow I will lay thee low!"

"Since it must be so," quoth Earl Percy, "to whom shall I yield?"

"Thou shalt not yield to me or to any lord, but to the bracken bush that grows on yonder lea!"

"I will not yield to briar or bracken bush, but I would yield to Lord Douglas or to Sir Hugh Montgomery, if he were here."

Then Montgomery made himself known, and as soon as Percy knew that it was Montgomery, he struck the point of his sword into the ground, and Montgomery, who was a courteous knight, took him up by the hand.

This deed was done at Otterbourne at daybreak, where Earl Douglas was buried by the bracken bush, and Percy led captive into Scotland, and it is said that Hotspur, for his ransom, built for Montgomery the castle of Penoon, in Ayrshire.

But the English version of these stirring events can also claim to be heard; the ballad upon it is called *Chevy Chase*, which means the Chase on the Cheviots; and so popular was this ballad that its name was given to a boys' game, which is so called even to this day. It tells how the Percy, from his castle in Northumberland, vowed that within three days he would hunt on the mountains of Cheviot in spite of the doughty Douglas and his men, and that he would kill and carry away the fattest deer in Cheviot.

"By my faith," said Douglas, when he heard of the boast, "but I will hinder his hunting."

Percy left Bamborough Castle with a mighty company, no less than fifteen hundred bold archers chosen out of three shires.

The foray began on a Monday morning in the high Cheviot Hills, and many a child yet unborn was to rue the day.

The drivers went through the woods and raised the deer, and the bowmen shot them with their broad arrows. Then the wild deer rushed through the woods, only to be met and killed by the greyhounds, and before noontide a hundred fat deer lay dead. The bugles sounded, " A mort ! " and on all sides Percy and his men assembled to see the cutting up of the venison.

Said Percy : " The Douglas promised to meet me here this day, yet right well did I know that he would fail." But a Northumberland squire saw the doughty Douglas coming with a mighty company, with spear and batter-axe and sword. Never were men hardier of heart and hand seen in Christendom—two thousand spearmen born along the banks of the Tweed and Teviotdale. Then said Lord Percy : " Now leave off the cutting of the deer, and take good heed to your bows, for never had ye more need of them since ye were born."

Earl Douglas rode before his men, his armour glittering like a burning coal, and never was such a bold baron. " Tell me whose men ye are," said he, " and who gave ye leave to hunt in Cheviot without word asked of me ? "

Then answered Lord Percy, " We will not tell thee whose men we are, and we will hunt here in spite of thee. We have killed the fattest harts in Cheviot and will carry them away."

" By my troth," said Douglas, " one of us shall die this day. Yet it were great pity to kill all these guiltless men. Thou, Percy, art a lord of land, and I am called an earl in my country ; let our men stand by, and we will fight together."

" Now a curse on his crown, who says nay to that," cried Lord Percy. " By my troth, Douglas, thou shalt never see the day either in England, Scotland, or France, when I fear to meet one, man to man."

Then spoke Richard Witherington, a squire of Northumberland. " Never shall this be told in England, to the shame of good King Harry the Fourth. I wot ye be two great lords, and I but a poor squire, yet would I never stand and look on while my captain fought. While I can wield a weapon, I will not fail, both heart and hand."

So the English with good heart bent their bows, and slew seven score spearmen with the first arrows they shot.

Earl Douglas stayed on the field, but that he was a good captain was truly seen, for he wrought great woe and mischief. He parted his host in three like a proud chieftain, and they came in on every side with their mighty spears, wounding the English archers and slaying many a brave man.

Then the English pulled out their brands, and it was a heavy sight to see the bright swords light on the helmets, striking through the rich mail, and the cloth of many folds under it, and laying many low.

At last the Douglas and the Percy met and fought with swords of Milan steel till the blood spurted like rain and hail from their helmets.

"Hold thee, Percy," said Douglas, "and I will bring thee to James, our Scottish king, where thou shalt have an earl's wages and free ransom, for thou art the manfullest man that ever yet I conquered fighting in the field."

"Nay, then," said Lord Percy. "I told thee before that never would I yield to any man of woman born."

With that there came an arrow hastily from a mighty man, and struck Earl Douglas through the breast bone, and never more did he speak a word but only this: "Fight, my merry men, while ye may—my life's days are done."

Then Percy leaned on his hand, and when he saw the Douglas die, he said, "Woe is me. I would have parted with my land for three years to have saved thy life, for a better man of heart and hand was not in all the north country."

But Sir Hugh Montgomery, a Scottish knight, when he saw the Douglas done to death, grasped a spear and rode through a hundred archers, never slackening his pace till he came to Lord Percy, whom he set upon, sending his mighty spear clean through his body, so that a man might see a long cloth-yard and more at the other side. There were no two better captains in Christendom than were that day slain.

When one of the Northumberland archers saw this, he drew an arrow to his bow and set upon Montgomery, until the swan feathers of his arrows were wet with his heart's blood.

Not one man gave way, but still they stood hewing at each other, while they were able.

This battle began in Cheviot, an hour before noon, nor was it half done at evensong, but they fought on by moonlight though many had scarce the strength to stand. Of fifteen hundred English archers only fifty-three remained, and of two thousand Scottish spearmen only fifty-five remained, all the rest being slain in Cheviot.

With Lord Percy were slain, Sir John of Agerstone, Sir Roger the gentle Hartly, Sir William the bold Heron, Sir George the worthy Lovel, a renowned knight, and Sir Ralph the rich Rugby. Woe was it that Witherington was slain, for when both his legs were hewn in two he kneeled and fought on his knees.

With the brave Douglas were slain Sir Hugh Montgomery, and worthy Sir Davy Liddle, that was his sister's son; Sir Charles, a Murray who refused to flee, and Sir Hugh Maxwell. On the morrow they made biers of birch and grey hazel, and many widows bore weeping from the field the bodies of their dead husbands. Well may Teviotdale and Northumberland wail and moan for two such great captains.

Word came to James the Scottish king at Edinburgh, that the brave Douglas, Lieutenant of the Marches, lay slain in Cheviot, and he wept and wrung his hands, and said, " Alas ! Woe is me; there will never be such another captain in Scotland."

Word came also to London, to Harry the Fourth, that Lord Percy, Lieutenant of the Marches, lay slain in Cheviot. " God have mercy on his soul," said King Harry; " I have a hundred captains in England as good as he, yet I wager my life that his death shall be well avenged " ; and this vow he kept, at the Battle of Homildon Hill, where he beat down six and thirty Scottish knights on one day.

But so real to the Borderers was their grief over their dead that the ballad ends with a quaint but heartfelt appeal to the Prince of Peace :—

" Jesus Christ our ills abate,
And to His bliss us bring !
Thus was the hunting of the Cheviot;
God send us all good ending !"

Chapter XII

The Douglas Clan

THE Douglas clan was at one time the strongest of all the great Scotch families on the Border; they were wild and proud and recklessly brave, and no account of the Borders would be complete without the broad details of their tragic history.

The first to raise the fame of the family to the highest place in honour was the brave Sir James Douglas, the friend of Bruce, and, after Bruce himself, the greatest hero among the Scots of that stormy period. He was a powerful, black-haired man with a dark complexion, and was called by the English "The Black Douglas." So great was the terror of his name that English mothers on the Border, when their children were naughty, would tell them that the Black Douglas would get them, or if they were fretful they would comfort them with the assurance—

"Hush ye, hush ye, little pet ye,
Hush ye, hush ye, do not fret ye,
The Black Douglas shall not get ye."

Sir Walter Scott relates how, when the garrison of Roxburgh Castle were making merry at Shrovetide, the castle was surprised by the Douglas, who mounted to the ramparts where a woman was crooning the refrain to her babe. "You are not so sure of that," he said, laying his hand upon her shoulder. It is pleasant to read that on this occasion the Black Douglas did not turn out so black as he was painted, and beyond her fright the woman came to no harm at the hands of Sir James and his followers.

At one time the English had seized the Douglas castle in Lanarkshire, and Sir James and his men disguised themselves and came to church on Palm Sunday, when the English soldiers were worshipping there. Suddenly in the midst of the service Douglas dropped his cloak and drew his sword and shouted: "A Douglas! a Douglas!"

The English soldiers were taken by surprise, and were killed before they could recover themselves. This deed brought Douglas great fame, but after all it was hardly a fair fight.

In 1327, when Edward III. was only fifteen years old, Douglas led a raid into Northumberland and Durham which did the English much damage. Edward came after them with an English army, and the Scots, being outnumbered, were compelled to dodge up and down in order to avoid a pitched battle. But in one bold night attack, Douglas and five hundred of the Scots penetrated to the king's tent, and almost succeeded in taking him prisoner. Failing in this, they returned unharmed to their own country, and shortly afterwards, at the Treaty of Northampton in 1328, King Edward III. agreed to acknowledge Robert Bruce as King of Scotland, and the long war between Scotland and England ended.

A year later Bruce died, but after a romantic custom of that day he bequeathed his heart to his gallant friend, Sir James Doulgas. Douglas had this heart enclosed in a silver casket and carried it hung about his neck. The war with England being over, this restless knight sought adventures in Spain, fighting against the Saracen followers of Mahomet. In one fierce battle, he and his men were surrounded by their enemies. Douglas, probably realising that this was his last fight, took the casket and flung it into the midst of his foes, crying: "Go first in fight, as thou wert used to do; Douglas will follow thee or die!" He then rushed desperately after it, fighting his way on till at last his dead body fell on this dearly prized relic, which he guarded to the end. The casket lies buried in the Abbey of Melrose, but Douglas's body was laid in his own church.

Of the bold Earl Douglas who fought and died at Otterbourne the tale is told in our last chapter. We may pass on to another famous Douglas, this time a heroine, who lived in the reign of James I. of Scotland (quite a different king from James I. of England). When James was only twelve years old, he was taken prisoner by Henry IV. of England, and kept captive till he was thirty. But he was given an education fit for a king, and in England he met the lady he devotedly loved, Lady Joan Beaufort, daughter of the Earl of Somerset. He addressed a beautiful poem to her and married her, and these two always most dearly loved one another. When at last his long captivity came to an end, he got back to Scotland to find the kingdom in disorder, and the nobles defying the law and acting as they pleased. James, a strong and able king, set his strength against their strength, and gradually got his whole kingdom into order and ruled with wisdom and justice.

But in these days it was impossible to be firm without sternness, and James made enemies. When he was staying at Perth one Christmas-time, these enemies, led by a bold villain called Sir Robert Graham, secretly encircled the house where he was staying. The unarmed king only heard of their presence when they were advancing, fully armed, to his room. He tore up a plank in the floor, seeking thus to find a hiding-place. The enemies were almost at the door, and it was necessary to delay their entrance, for one minute might save his life. All the bars of the door had been removed beforehand, but a brave heroine, Kate Douglas, thrust her arm through the staples. The villains were angered to find the door barred against them, and hurled their weight upon it.

The Douglas heroine stood there, her pale face set hard, without a cry, as the crash broke the bone of her brave strong arm, and the would-be murderers staggered in. But alas! the sacrifice of Kate Douglas availed nothing except to place her name upon the immortal roll of the heroes of the ages, for after a brief search the murderers found the king and slew him.

The queen, who had loved James with the utmost devotion, found her love give added fierceness to her hate against his murderers. They were all tracked down, and she caused them to die with terrible tortures, the cruellest of which she reserved for Graham. Thus did great King James's "milk-white dove" revenge the slaying of the husband she loved dearer than life itself.

Till this time it had seemed as if the Douglases were devoted to the good of Scotland. But in those wild, reckless times qualities that were strong for good could also be strong for evil.

When James I. of Scotland was murdered, his young son was only six years old. This meant that for many years there would be no strong king able to cope with the lawless spirit of the nobles, strongest among whom were the proud, bold Douglases.

The lawlessness of the times is well shown by an act of foul treachery committed by Sir William Crichton, Governor of Edinburgh, and an enemy of the Douglas family. He invited one of the earls to dinner at the castle, and while there had him seized and beheaded. It is said that a bull's head was placed on the dish in front of Douglas, this being a sign that he was to be killed. The people called this "Douglas's black dinner," and sang of the wicked deed in sorrowful verse :—

> "Edinburgh Castle, town and tower
> God grant thou sink for sin !
> And even for that black dinner
> Earl Douglas got therein."

But the new King James found, before he was twenty years old, that the Douglases themselves could act with equal cruelty and lawlessness.

The king was fond of a brave young soldier named Maclellan, who, having some quarrel with Earl Douglas, was thrown by him into a dungeon in his castle. So the king wrote a letter to Douglas, saying he must set Maclellan free, and sent this letter by Maclellan's uncle, Sir Patrick Gray. When Douglas saw Gray riding up to his castle, he at once guessed the errand. So he came out as though he were delighted to see him, and insisted on his sitting down and having dinner with him, before the king's letter was opened and discussed. But the treacherous earl had given secret orders that Maclellan should be beheaded while they were dining, so that after dinner was over, and the letter was read, he could say that this had been done before he had seen the king's message.

Gray dared not show his anger, for fear he too should be killed. He mounted his swift horse and rode away, but the moment he was outside the castle walls he shook his mailed fist at Douglas and cried out—

"Treacherous earl, disgrace to knighthood, some day you shall pay for this black, base deed ! "

Douglas mounted his men, and they pursued Gray almost to the gates of Edinburgh; but he rode for his life, and faster than they.

When Douglas and the king next met there was a stormy scene. The earl was so proud and wilful that he would not bend to any of the king's wishes or heed the king's anger in the least. So King James, mad with rage, stabbed the reckless earl with his dagger, and Sir Patrick Gray, seeing this, struck him a death-blow with his axe.

The king was in Stirling Castle, a powerful fortress at the top of a steep hill, when the new earl, the younger brother of the murdered man, rode up with six hundred followers, and burnt and plundered the town before the king's very eyes, and added to the insult by publicly declaring that King James II. was a law-breaker.

For three years the quarrel went on between the king and the Douglases, but it was then evident that there could be no peace between them. So at last the king's army attacked the collected forces of the strong Douglas family at a place on the Borders then called Arkinholm, where the picturesque little town of Langholm now stands. Here the beautiful river Esk receives the water of two smaller streams, and so it was a good place to make a stand for a fight. The battle was long and desperate; three brothers of the bold black Douglases were there, and they withstood the king's men till the rivers ran red; but their cause was hopeless. One was slain in battle; one was taken and executed; one escaped into England; and the power of the Black Douglases was gone.

Thus it was that the strongest and most famous family of the Borders was broken up, because its proud leaders dared to dictate to the king himself.

Chapter XIII

Alnwick Castle and the Percies

THE castle of Alnwick stands on a hill on the south bank of the river Alne; being protected on one side by the river and on another by a deep gorge, it stands in a strong natural position. There are traces of earthworks that seem to show that the spot was fortified in the old British days, but the earliest fact which we know certainly is that there was a Saxon fortress here, held by a Gilbert Tyson, when William the Conqueror claimed England. Tyson hastened south to fight on Harold's side, and was killed at the battle of Hastings.

The fortress seems to have got into the hands of a Norman knight, Ivo de Vesci, who married the grand-daughter of Gilbert Tyson. King Malcolm of Scotland was killed in front of it, in 1093, with three thousand of his men. De Vesci's son-in-law was probably the knight who rebuilt the castle in the Norman style, some portions of which still remain.

In 1174, William the Lion, King of Scotland, who had claimed Northumberland as his own, attacked the castles of Wark and of Alnwick. Wark was defended by a gallant knight named Roger de Stuteville. William's brave men tried in vain to force their way through the portcullis, but were beaten back. Then William ordered up his *perière*, a machine made for hurling stones. "This," said the king, "will soon smash down the gate for us!" With great expectations the machine was set in motion, but it acted so badly that it threw the stones on to William's own men, and nearly killed one of his best knights! William raved in his fury, and swore he would rather have been captured in fair fight than be made to look so foolish in the eyes of his enemies. He gave word to burn the castle, but the wind was in the wrong quarter and blew back the flames. So he had to give up the siege. Stuteville, like a gallant enemy, told his men not to shout taunts and jeers at the departing Scots. But instead they blew trumpets and horns, and sang songs, and called out a very loud and hearty "Good-bye."

Shortly afterwards, William came before Alnwick, and it was then De Vesci's turn. It was Saturday morning on a hot July day, and the Scottish king's knights flatteringly told him that the English were bound to give way to him, and Northumberland would be his. The king was dining in front of the castle, with no helmet on, when suddenly a part of the English army made a surprise attack. The bold king leapt on to his grey charger, and unhorsed the first knight he met. So quick and brave were the Scots that they had almost defeated the English when an English foot-soldier stabbed the king's horse with his lance, and it fell, bringing William down to the ground and pinning him there. This turned the course of battle; the Scots were beaten back, and William taken prisoner.

In was in 1309 that the great Percy family first obtained possession of Alnwick and its domain. Henry Percy purchased it from Anthony Bek, Bishop of Durham, who had somehow obtained power over it, and the brave De Vesci family disappear. About this date Northumberland was in a miserable condition; it was the reign of the feeble Edward II., and Bruce had invaded the four northernmost counties of England, and was exacting tribute from them. The English were safe only within their fortresses.

However, the brave Sir Thomas Gray, who held Norham Castle, did much to uphold the falling honour of England, and Henry Percy almost rebuilt the castle of Alnwick, which in his son's time successfully withstood a siege. But at last peace was restored by the Treaty of Northampton in 1328, by the terms of which the English king renounced all claim to Scotland.

The Percy family were of Norman origin, deriving their name from a Norman village. William de Percy crossed to England just after the battle of Hastings, and received grants of land in Yorkshire. Agnes de Percy married Jocelin, Count of Louvain, and their son Henry took his mother's surname. From that year onward, the the Christian name of Henry was always given to the eldest son; there were fourteen Henry Percies!

Even in these wild times the Percies were distinguished by the boldness of their spirits. One of the Counts of Louvain, grandfather of the first Henry Percy, shocked the men of his day by hanging some of his enemies with the church bell-ropes. It was not the hanging that was objected to—hanging was common enough; but the use of church-ropes for the purpose was thought very wicked!

After they had rebuilt Alnwick Castle and settled down there, the Percies soon established their power in the North. At the coronation of Richard II., in 1377, a Henry Percy was Marshal of England, and he was then made Earl of Northumberland. His son, "Hotspur," was the most famous of all the Percies. In their time, the battles of Otterbourne and Homildon Hill were fought. But they rebelled against Henry IV. and Hotspur was killed at the battle of Shrewsbury (1403), while his father was slain a few years later at Bramham Moor, his head set up on London Bridge, and quarters of his body on the gates of Berwick, Newcastle, Lincoln, and London, to discourage others from following in his footsteps!

Henry, son of "Hotspur," was the second earl. He repaired and added to the castle and was present at the battle of Agincourt. It was not the habit of the Percies to die in their beds, and this one was killed in the Wars of the Roses, at the first battle of St Albans, in 1455.

The fact of their having taken the losing Lancastrian side in these wars kept the family under a cloud for a number of years. One of them deserted Richard III. on Bosworth field in 1485; one of them was beheaded at York in 1572, for taking part in the "Rising of the North"; one of them was found shot in his bed in 1585, and another died in the Tower in 1632. So that the family could hardly be said to be quieting down.

They sided with Parliament during the Civil War, but later on they favoured the Restoration. At last there came a time when there were no male heirs left in this great line, but only a daughter, Elizabeth. She married the Duke of Somerset, and had thirteen children, the eldest surviving of whom was created Earl of Northumberland in 1748. But he died the year after, leaving only a daughter, who had married a very able baronet, to whom was given the title of Duke of Northumberland in 1766. He very wisely took the surname of Percy, and again restored the castle of Alnwick, putting the family estates and affairs in good order. So that the Percies of Alnwick Castle are Dukes of Northumberland to this day.

Chapter XIV

Hexham and Queen Margaret

THE town of Hexham stands on the south bank of the Tyne, rising gradually up the hill and presenting a most picturesque appearance. About two miles above Hexham the North and the South Tyne meet, and the combined river is broad and noble, and the hills around Hexham give strength and beauty to the scene. The commanding appearance and central position of the priory church adds its note of dignity, and the total effect of the town is very pleasing to the eye.

There is no doubt that from very early times there was a town in this fine natural position. The burial-grounds of primitive races have been discovered here, with stone and bronze implements. The Romans had a town here of some importance, although it was four miles south of their great wall. A Roman tombstone was discovered here, nine feet by three and a half feet, showing a Roman officer on horseback, overthrowing in fierce fight a savage and scowling foe. This fine relic is sent up in the church, and is not the only thing to see there. The original church upon this spot was built in 674, in the reign of King Egfrid of Northumbria. Wilfrid, the very able and influential Bishop of York, was the man who presided at the building of it, and there were bishops at Hexham for a couple of centuries. In

875 the Danes ruthlessly burnt the town; and nearly one thousand years later, in 1832, there was found buried in the ground a bronze vessel containing about nine thousand Saxon coins of the eighth and ninth century, evidently buried to protect this treasure from the invaders. Those who buried them were probably slain before they had time to dig them up again. There was a legend of another treasure hidden between Hexham and Corbridge, and King John came to Hexham in 1201 to search for it. He returned in 1208 and in 1212, but found nothing. Time passed, and this tale of hidden treasure ceased even to be local gossip, but in 1735 by accident it was found.

The present handsome priory church must have been built about the time of King John's visits to Hexham. It is a noble building, well worth a visit. In 1725, when some work was being done in the church, a wonderful discovery was made. It was found that there was an old Saxon crypt, a narrow vault with several passages, underneath the church! This was so carefully hidden that it was evidently intended as a place of refuge in danger. It was built of Roman stones, several of which have Roman inscriptions.

The Scots several times attacked Hexham. Once Sir William Wallace came there with his army, but he would not let his Scots damage the church, so that Hexham, on the whole, had a less stormy life than many of the Border towns, although in 1537, when Henry VIII. caused the monastery to be suppressed, the prior and five of the leading monks were hanged before the gates as a gentle reminder that they were to live there no longer.

But by far the most stirring event in Hexham's history was the battle which raged there in 1464. The Wars of the Roses do not form a pleasing episode in English history. They were pitiless, and treachery was mingled with bloodshed; desertions and executions were the accompaniment of every battle. Edward IV. was coldly cruel and unscrupulous, one of the blackest figures of a black time. But romance centres round Queen Margaret, the dauntless and resourceful wife of the feeble King Henry VI., with whom Edward disputed the throne. She it was who, making up for her husband's weakness, urged ever bravely and hopefully the cause of her son. Thus she pressed on to the very end, till that son, worthy of his heroic mother, proudly answered the taunts of his base enemies, even though in their power, preferring speedy death to any lessening of his tragic dignity, and dying before the eyes of the successful and exultant Edward.

In this fierce drama, Hexham was but an episode. The Lancastrians had scattered after their heavy defeat at Towton. Margaret in person had begged a little help of the King of Scotland, a little more of the King of France. The Borderland was favourable to her, and she gathered her forces together there, King Henry VI. staying in Alnwick Castle.

Lord Montague, brother to the powerful but crafty Earl of Warwick, was warden of the East Marches for Edward, and he hastily collected the Yorkist forces. He was swift, able, and unscrupulous. He attacked a small body of Lancastrians on Hedgeley Moor, only ten miles from Alnwick, and defeated them, killing their leader, Sir Ralph Percy, son of Hotspur. As this gallant man died he consoled himself by saying, "I have saved the bird in my bosom," by which poetical phrase he meant that he had saved his honour by being true to his queen. In May the greater battle of Hexham was fought. King

Henry was there in person, with the dauntless Queen Margaret and her son, and their brave general, the Duke of Somerset. They marched out of Hexham to attack Lord Montague; the battle began by the village of Linnels, on the south side of the Devil's Water, a stream that runs into the Tyne. The fight was desperate, for both sides knew that no quarter would be given. It is said by some that the Scots, having no interest in the war, deserted Margaret; anyway, bit by bit the Lancastrians were forced back, to the very streets of Hexham itself, two miles away. In these narrow streets, in the quarter that is still called Battle Hill, the last desperate fighters on the side of the Red Rose made their final and unavailing stand.

At last the remnant fled, and no doubt many a Hexham maid and dame, at the risk of her own life or limb, hid that day some devoted follower of Margaret.

The gallant Duke of Somerset was taken prisoner, and there and then was brought to the block in the market-place and beheaded. The cruel Montague had not the true soldier's respect for a brave enemy, whose blood thus mingled with that of his men. Other nobles were taken as prisoners to Newcastle, but Edward also was devoid of mercy, and all perished.

Till the last moment the queen hoped on. She was not daunted by scenes of strife and bloodshed. When defeat was an accomplished fact, she and her young son fled to the Dipton Woods, where they fell into the hands of rough men, some say a party of Yorkist stragglers. Whilst these men were eagerly dividing and quarrelling over the queen's jewels, she and the prince slipped away. Deeper into the dangerous woods they had to go, for worse than robbers were hunting for them around Hexham. Suddenly an outlaw stood in their path with

The Final Battle in the Streets of Hexham

drawn sword. Even after that day of stir and terror Margaret's courage did not fail her. She boldly declared to the man that she was the Queen of England, and with her was her only son. Now, if he chose to betray them he could do so; but if he had that natural nobility that hailed gladly great chances to do great deeds, now was his time to prove himself a man, and to save the ill-fated prince and his queen.

The robber bowed before her as though she were on her throne, and as if the trees were her army around her. He swore to die a hundred deaths rather than betray his rightful sovereign and her prince. He honourably kept his word; and through his safe guidance and steady devotion, both queen and prince were able to join King Henry in Scotland, to which place he had safely escaped.

Thus the bandit of Hexham proved himself to be a truer man than either Lord Montague, or Warwick, the King-maker, or King Edward IV. of England.

Chapter XV

Fair Helen of Kirkconnell

VERY simple, very touching, is the story of fair Helen of Kirkconnell. This beautiful maiden had two lovers, one rich, one poor. Her friends favoured the rich one, she loved the poor one. She and her chosen lover used to meet secretly in the romantic churchyard of Kirkconnell, by the side of the river Kirtle. Learning this, the rejected lover crept up one evening, with his carbine, to shoot his luckier rival; Helen saw him at the moment of firing, and threw herself forward to receive the shot in her bosom, and so save her lover's life at the cost of her own.

The ballad describing the grief of her lover is one of the most beautiful and touching pieces of poetry in existence, and must be given here entire.

FAIR HELEN

I wish I were where Helen lies;
Night and day on me she cries;
O that I were where Helen lies,
On fair Kirkconnell Lee!

Curst be the heart that thought the thought,
And curst the hand that shot the shot,

When in my arms burd Helen dropt,
And died to succour me.

O think ye not my heart was sair,
When my love dropt and spak nae mair!
There did she swoon wi' meikle care,
On fair Kirkconnell Lee.

As I went down the water-side,
None but my foe to be my guide,
None but my foe to be my guide,
On fair Kirkconnell Lee!

I lighted down my sword to draw,
I hacked him in pieces sma',
I hacked him in pieces sma',
For her sake that died for me.

O Helen fair beyond compare,
I'll make a garland of thy hair,
Shall bind my heart for evermair,
Until the day I die.

O that I were where Helen lies,
Night and day on me she cries;
Out of my bed she bids me rise,
Says, "Haste and come to me!"

O Helen fair! O Helen chaste!
If I were with thee, I were blest,
Where thou lies low, and takes thy rest,
On fair Kirkconnell Lee.

O that my grave were growing green,
A winding sheet drawn ower my een,
And I in Helen's arms were lying,
    On fair Kirkconnell Lee!

I wish I were where Helen lies!
Night and day on me she cries,
And I am weary of the skies,
    For her sake that died for me.

Chapter XVI

Johnie of Breadislee

JOHNIE of Breadislee, outlaw and deer-stealer, was one of the "broken men," as they were called, the Ishmaels of the Border. Johnie rose up one May morning, and called for water to wash his hands. He ordered to be unleashed his good grey dogs, that were bound with iron chains. When his mother heard that he had called for the dogs, she wrung her hands. "O Johnie!" she cried, "for my blessing, do not go to the greenwood to-day. Ye have enough of good wheat bread, enough blood-red wine, therefore, Johnie, I pray, stir not from home for any venison." But despite his mother's tears, Johnie busked up his good bent bow, and his arrows, and went off to Durrisdeer to hunt down the dun deer. As he came by Merriemass he espied a deer lying beneath a bush of furze. Johnie let fly an arrow, and the deer leapt as the pitiless shaft found its mark, and between the water and the brae his good hounds "laid her pride." So Johnie cut up the venison, giving the liver and lungs to his faithful hounds, as if they had been earl's sons. With such zest did they eat and drink that Johnie and the dogs fell asleep, as if they had been dead. Then as they lay, there came by a silly old man, and, as soon as he saw the poachers, he ran away to Hislinton, where the Seven Foresters were. "What news?" they asked. "What news bring ye, ye grey-headed carle ?" "I bring no news," said the grey-headed carle, "save what my eyes did see. As I came down by Merrimass among the stunted trees, the bonniest child I ever saw lay asleep among his dogs. The shirt upon his back was of fine Holland, his doubtlet, over that, was of Lincoln twine, his buttons were of the good gold, the mouths of his good grey hounds were dyed with blood."

Now Johnie, like many another free-hearted outlaw, was a well-liked man. So the chief forester said, "If this be Johnie of Breadislee we will draw no nearer." But this was not the spirit of his men. Quoth the sixth Forester, "If it indeed be he, rather let us slay him." Cautiously they went through the thicket, and when they saw their man, asleep and helpless, they shot a flight of arrows. Johnie sprang up, sore wounded on the knee. The seventh forester cried out, "The next flight will kill him," but little chance did the outlaw give them for such an easy victory. He set his back against an oak and propped his wounded leg upon a stone; with bow or with sword he was a better man by far than any of his foes.

In the short, sharp fight that followed, he killed six of the foresters, some with arrow, and some with steel; and when the seventh turned to flee, Johnie seized him from behind and threw him on to the ground with a force that broke three of his ribs. Then he laid him on his steed, and bade him carry the tidings home.

But Johnie himself was hurt to death. "Is there no bonnie singing bird," he cried, "that can fly to my mother's bower and tell her to fetch Johnie away ?" A starling flew to his mother's window sill, and sang and whistled, and the burden of its tune was ever the same. "Johnie tarries long." So the men made a litter from

H Johnie of Breadislee

rods of the hazel bush and of the thorn and fetched Johnie away. Then his old mother's tears flowed fast, and she said, "Ye would not be warned, my son Johnie, to bide away from the hunting. Oft have I brought to Breadislee the less or greater gear, but never what grieved my heart so sorely. But woe betide that silly old grey-headed carle! An ill death shall he die! The highest tree in Merriemass shall be his reward."

"Now Johnie's gude bent bow is brake,
And his gude grey dogs are slain,
And his body lies dead in Durrisdeer,
And his hunting it is done."

Chapter XVII

Katharine Janfarie

THIS ballad is evidently the original of Sir Walter Scott's "Lochinvar," though Sir Walter reversed the names of the two leading male characters. In "Katharine Janfarie" Lochinvar plays the part of the craven bridegroom.

There was a may,[1] and a weel-far'd may,
Lived high up in yon glen;
Her name was Katharine Janfarie,
She was courted by mony men.

Up there came Lord Lauderdale,
Up frae the Lowland Border,
And he has come to court this may,
A' mounted in good order.

He told na her father, he told na her mother,
And he told na ane o' her kin,
But he whispered the bonnie lassie hersell,
And has her favour won.

But out there cam Lord Lochinvar,
Out frae the English Border,

[1] maiden.

All for to court this bonny may,
  Weel mounted, and in order.

He told her father, he told her mother,
  And a' the lave [1] o' her kin;
But he told na the bonny may hersell,
  Till on her wedding e'en.

She sent to the Lord o' Lauderdale,
  Gin [2] he wad come and see,
And he has sent back word again,
  Weel answered he suld [3] be.

And he has sent a messenger
  Right quickly through the land,
And raised mony an armed man
  To be at his command.

The bride looked out at a high window,
  Beneath baith dale and down,
And she was aware of her first true love,
  With riders mony a one.

She scoffed him, and scorned him,
  Upon her wedding-day;
And said, "It was the Fairy Court,
  To see him in array!

"O come ye here to fight, young lord,
  Or come ye here to play?
Or come ye here to drink good wine,
  Upon the wedding-day?"

[1] rest. [2] if. [3] should.

"I come na here to fight," he said,
  "I come na here to play,
I'll but lead a dance wi' the bonny bride,
  And mount, and go my way."

It is a glass of the blood-red wine
  Was filled up them between,
And aye she drank to Lauderdale,
  Wha [1] her true love had been.

He's taen [2] her by the milk-white hand,
  And by the grass-green sleeve;
He's mounted her hie behind himsell,
  At her kinsmen speired [3] na leave.

"Now take your bride, Lord Lochinvar!
  Now take her if ye may!
But if you take your bride again,
  We'll call it but foul play."

There were four-and-twenty bonnie boys,
  A' clad in the Johnstone grey;
They said they would take the bride again,
  By the strong hand, if they may.

Some o' them were right willing men,
  But they were na willing a';
And four-and-twenty Leader lads
  Bid them mount and ride awa'.

Then whingers flew frae gentles' sides,
  And swords flew frae the shea's,[4]
And red and rosy was the blood
  Ran down the lily braes.

[1] who [2] taken. [3] asked. [4] sheathes.

The blood ran down by Caddon bank,
And down by Caddon brae,
And, sighing, said the bonnie bride—
" O wae's me for foul play."

My blessing on your heart, sweet thing!
Wae to your wilfu' will!
There's mony a gallant gentleman
Whae's bluid ye have garred [1] to spill.

Now a' the lords of fair England,
And that dwell by the English Border,
Come never here to seek a wife,
For fear of sic [2] disorder.

They'll track ye up, and settle ye bye,
Till on your wedding-day;
Then gie ye frogs instead of fish,
And play ye foul foul play.

LOCHINVAR

In Sir Walter Scott's poem, Lochinvar is the hero, and the story has a happier ending. The song was supposed to have been sung to James IV. by Lady Heron at Holyrood shortly before the fatal battle of Flodden.

O young Lochinvar has come out of the west,
Through all the wide border his steel was the best;
And save his good broadsword, he weapons had none,
He rode all unarmed, and he rode all alone,
So faithful in love, and so dauntless in war,
There never was knight like the young Lochinvar.

[1] caused. [2] such.

He staid not for brake, and he stopped not for stone,
He swam the Eske river where ford there was none,
But ere he alighted at Netherby gate,
The bride had consented, the gallant came late;
For a laggard in love, and a dastard in war,
Was to wed the fair Ellen of brave Lochinvar.

So boldly he entered the Netherby Hall,
Among bride's men, and kinsmen, and brothers, and all,
Then spoke the bride's father, his hand on his sword
(For the poor craven bridegroom said never a word),
"O come ye in peace here, or come ye in war,
Or to dance at our bridal, young Lord Lochinvar?"

"I long wooed your daughter, my suit you denied;
Love swells like the Solway, but ebbs like its tide,
And now am I come, with this lost love of mine,
To lead but one measure, drink one cup of wine,
There are maidens in Scotland, more lovely by far,
That would gladly be bride to the young Lochinvar."

The bride kissed the goblet; the knight took it up,
He quaffed off the wine, and he threw down the cup.
She looked down to blush, and she looked up to sigh,
With a smile on her lips, and a tear in her eye.
He took her soft hand, ere her mother could bar,
"Now tread we a measure!" said young Lochinvar.

So stately her form, and so lovely her face,
That never a hall such a galliard did grace;
While her brother did fret, and her father did fume,
And the bridgroom stood dangling his bonnet and plume,
And the bride-maidens whispered, "'Twere better by far,
To have matched our fair cousin with young Lochinvar."

One touch to her hand, and one word in her ear,
When they reached the hall-door, and the charger stood
near;
So light to the croupe the fair lady he swung,
So light to the saddle before her he sprung!
"She is won! we have gone over bank, bush, and scaur;
They'll have fleet steeds that follow," quoth young
Lochinvar.

There was mounting 'mong Græmes of the Netherby
clan;
Fosters, Fenwicks, and Musgraves, they rode and they
ran,
There was racing and chasing, on Cannobie Lee,
But the lost bride of Netherby ne'er did they see.
So daring in love, and so dauntless in war,
Have ye e'er heard of gallant like young Lochinvar?

Chapter XVIII

By Lauder Bridge

THE Ancient Royal Burgh of Lauder, a quaint little border town with hardly more than one street, is on the banks of the river Leader, on the high road between Edinburgh and Kelso. It stands very picturesquely, among the bold hills and fine woods of Berwickshire, and the valley is called Lauderdale, extending to where the Leader joins the Tweed, just below Melrose. Peacefully beautiful is the spot; and yet it was once the scene of a harsh, grim tragedy.

It was in the reign of King James III. of Scotland, who offended his subjects in two particulars.

First, to get wealth for himself, he mixed brass and lead with his silver money, and put it into circulation as pure silver; next, he chose favourites from the common people, and set these above the proud noblemen of Scotland.

This latter would not have been so bad a fault if the king had always chosen wisely; but, as often in such cases, he was led by flatterers rather than by worthy men.

In 1482 the king declared war against England, and, as in these warlike days the nobles were the leaders of the army, this brought the discontented lords together.

When the Scottish army reached Lauder in their southward march, the proud nobles met in Lauder church; all were angry with the king, yet each was afraid to make the first move. So Lord Gray told them a mocking fable.

"Do you remember," said he, "how all the mice got together and agreed that it would be a splendid thing if a bell were hung round the cat's neck, so that wherever she went she could be heard; the only difficulty was to find a mouse to bell the cat!"

These warlike nobles did not like to be spoken of as if they were mice, and it roused them to deeper rage.

Then out spoke Archibald Douglas, Earl of Angus, the head of the younger branch of the Douglas family. "Trust me, I'll bell the cat!"

There was a knock at the door; Cochrane, the architect, whom the nobles said had been a mason, but was now the king's chief favourite, entered, dressed in black velvet, with a heavy chain of gold round his neck, a horn of gold tipped with precious stones, and all his attire of the costliest. Angus caught the chain in his hands and said, "A rope would suit that neck better!"

Then the nobles laid violent hands on all the king's low-born favourites and hanged them by the bridge of Lauder, in front of the king's very eyes! Cochrane was proud and brave to the last. He said that as the king had made him an earl he should be hanged with a rope made of silk; little did the nobles care for his protests, the halter of a horse was in their opinion good enough for him.

From this time onward the headstrong Earl of Angus was known by the nick-name of "Bell-the-Cat." It may be taken for granted that neither he nor the nobles who supported him would have dared to act so arrogantly and violently unless they felt quite sure that the king had not the power to punish them.

He returned sullenly to Edinburgh, more the captive of the nobles than their master.

A parliament appointed the Duke of Albany lieutenant-general of the kingdom, but he in turn soon lost favour, for he was suspected of too great a friendship for Edward IV., King of England, and fled for safety to France, giving James another chance to govern his kingdom for himself.

This weak and unhappy monarch, however, was not destined to have much peace. Before very long, another quarrel with his nobles led to their taking up arms with a view of deposing him and placing his son on the throne. The king and his nobles met in battle near Stirling, but, at the very beginning of the fight, James was thrown from his horse and stabbed by a soldier, whose name remained unknown. Thus died this weak but amiable and unfortunate king.

Chapter XIX

The Battle of Flodden Field

ONE of the most tragic episodes in the History of the Borders was the battle of Flodden Field, when the flower of the Scottish nobility fell around their sovereign, James IV., while fighting against the English under Surrey.

The causes of the war were many. Henry of England refused to give up the jewels which had been promised as the dowry of his sister Margaret on her marriage with James IV.

The Lord High Admiral of England, Sir Edmund Howard, had attacked and taken two Scottish ships, and slain their captain, Sir Andrew Barton. James, who was fond of Barton, demanded redress, but Henry insolently replied that kings should not quarrel about pirates.

But the immediate cause was the friendship between France and Scotland. Henry was preparing for war with France, and James stood by his ally, declaring that if Henry warred with France, he would lead an army into England. The Queen of France sent James a turquoise ring, asking him to carry out his threat to serve her interests.

James had been warned that his action would have terrible consequences. A man appeared to him at Linlithgow, clad in a long blue gown, with bare head, and carrying a pikestaff, and having told the king that his dead mother had sent him to warn him not to go to war against England, he disappeared as suddenly as he had come.

Also at the dead of night a voice had been heard proclaiming aloud at the market Cross in Edinburgh the names of those who, within forty days, would be no more. It was thought at the time that these happenings were instigated by Queen Margaret, but the king still persisted in his policy, and led his army across the Border, in spite of the warnings of his counsellors and his queen.

A fine description of his army is given by Sir Walter Scott, when Lord Marmion watches the scene from Blackford Hill.

"Thousand pavilions, white as snow,
Spread all the Borough-moor below,
Upland, and dale, and down :—
A thousand, did I say? I ween,
Thousands and thousands, there were seen,
That chequer'd all the heath between
The streamlet and the town;
In crossing ranks extending far,
Forming a camp irregular;
Oft giving way, where still there stood
Some relics of the old oak wood,
That darkly huge did intervene,
And tamed the glaring white with green;
In these extended lines there lay,
A martial kingdom's vast array.

For from Hebudes, dark with rain,
To eastern Lodon's fertile plain,
And from the southern Redswire edge,
To farthest Rosse's rocky ledge,
From west to east, from south to north,
Scotland sent all her warriors forth,

Marmion might hear the mingled hum,
Of myriads up the mountain come ;
The horses' tramp, and tingling clank,
Where chiefs reviewed their vassal rank,
  And charger's shrilling neigh ;
And see the shifting lines advance
Whilst frequent flash'd, from shield and lance,
  The sun's reflected ray.

. . . . .

They saw, slow rolling on the plain,
Full many a baggage-cart and wain,
And dire artillery's clumsy car.
By sluggish oxen tugg'd to war ;

. . . . .

Nor mark'd they less, where in the air
A thousand streamers flaunted fair,
  Various in shape, device, and hue,
  Green, sanguine, purple, red, and blue,
Broad, narrow, swallow-tailed, and square,
Scroll, pennon, pensil, bandrol,[1] there
  O'er the pavilions flew.
Highest and midmost, was descried
The royal banner floating wide ;
The staff, a pine-tree, strong and straight,
Pitch'd deeply in a massive stone,
Which still in memory is shown,
Yet bent beneath the standard's weight.
Whene'er the western breeze unroll'd,
With toil, the huge and cumbrous fold,
And gave to view the dazzling field,
Where, in proud Scotland's royal shield,
The ruddy lion ramp'd in gold."

Marmion wondered that with such a glorious army at his back anyone should try to dissuade James from battle, yet Sir David Lindesay of the Mount answered him,

[1] Each feudal ensign intimated the rank of those who displayed them.

> "'twere good
> That Kings would think withal,
> When peace and wealth their land has bless'd,
> 'Tis better to sit still at rest,
> Than rise, perchance to fall."

Men-at-arms were there, sheathed in plate armour, with battle-axe and spear, and mounted on Flemish steeds. Young knights and squires practised their chargers on the plain. Hardy burghers marched on foot, armed with long pikes and two-handed swords and bright bucklers.

The yeoman, too, was on foot, dressed in steel-jack quilted well with iron, and bearing at his back, provisions for forty days. He seemed sad of cheer, and loth to leave his humble cottage, wondering who would till the land during his absence.

There, too, was the Borderer :—

> "bred to war,
> He knew the battle's din afar,
> And joy'd to hear it swell.
> His peaceful day was slothful ease,
> Nor harp nor pipe his ear could please
> Like the loud slogan yell."

for

> "War's the Borderer's game,
> Their gain, their glory, their delight,
> To sleep the day, maraud the night,
> O'er mountain, moss, and moor."

There, too, were the Celts, with savage eyes looking out wildly through red and sable hair, with sinewy frames and legs bare above the knees, their chiefs known by the eagle's plumage. They wore the skin of the red deer, a graceful bonnet, and a plaid hung from the

Flodden Field

shoulders, and carried as weapons a broadsword, a dagger, and quivers, bows, and shafts.

The Isles-men, too, were there, carrying the ancient Danish battle-axe. While the army was mustering together, James feasted the chiefs in Holyrood Palace, for at dawn they were to march southward.

> "Well loved that splendid monarch aye
>   The banquet and the song,
> By day the tourney, and by night
> The merry dance, traced fast and light,
> The maskers quaint, the pageant bright,
>   The revel loud and long.
> This feast outshone his banquets past;
> It was his blithest and his last."
>
> And hazel was his eagle eye,
> And auburn of the darkest dye,
> His short curl'd beard and hair.
> Light was his footstep in the dance,
>   And firm his stirrup in the lists;
> And oh! he had that merry glance,
>   That seldom lady's heart resists."

Yet no fair lady was as dear to James as his own Queen Margaret, who sat alone in the tower of Linlithgow weeping for the war against her native country, and for the danger of her lord.

On the morrow, James marched south, crossed the Tweed, and encamped on the banks of the Till, near Twisel Bridge. The Scottish army moved down the side of the Tweed to Flodden Hill taking Norham Castle, and the Border towns of Etal, Wark, and Ford. Much time was wasted in these petty enterprises, time which should have been spent in marching to Newcastle before the English were prepared to offer resistance. When the castle of Ford was stormed, Lady Heron, wife of Sir

William Heron, then a prisoner in Scotland, was taken, and this beautiful and artful woman induced James to idle away his time until all chance was lost of defeating the enemy.

The army suffered severely from want of provisions, and many of the Highlanders and Isles-men returned home, many who had come only for booty, deserted, and the numbers were reduced to about thirty thousand.

Meanwhile, the Earl of Surrey had raised twenty-six thousand men, and received other enforcements as he came north from Durham. He therefore challenged James to fight, and charged him with violating the treaty of peace between the two kingdoms.

The Scottish nobles were unwilling to fight, and said it was impossible to remain in a country so plundered; also, if fight the king must, he would fight to much greater advantage in his own country, to whose welfare the loss of this battle would be fatal; while he had sufficiently indicated his honour by crossing the Border.

James would not listen to the counsel of his nobles, though even the aged Earl of Angus expostulated with him. To this old warrior he angrily said, "Angus, if you are afraid, you may go home," at which insult the aged Earl burst into tears.

The English army crossed the Till by Twisel Bridge and pressed on while the Scottish army stood idly by, the Scottish nobles in vain entreating the king to attack the English while they were crossing.

When the English army had drawn up in order of battle on the left bank of the river, the Scots, setting fire to their temporary huts, came down the ridge of Flodden. The clouds of smoke from the burning huts were driven into the face of the English, so that the Scots had got to within a quarter of a mile of them before they perceived them.

"No martial shout, nor minstrel tone,
Announced their march; their tread alone,
At times one warning trumpet blown,
At times a stifled hum,
Told England, from his mountain-throne,
King James did rushing come:
Scarce could they hear or see their foes
Until at weapon-point they close."

With clanging blows and arrows that fell like rain, with yelling and clamour and sword-sway and lance-thrust, the battle continued until the evening, and when even fell, the Scots still fought in an unbroken ring round their king. But when darkness came, and Surrey withdrew his men, the flower of Scotland's chivalry had fallen, and the king lay dead on the field.

"Afar, the royal standard flies,
And round it toils and bleeds and dies.
Our Caledonian pride!"

. . . . . .

But yet, though thick the shafts as now,
Though charging knights like whirlwinds go,
Though billmen ply the ghastly bow,
Unbroken was the ring.
The stubborn spearmen still made good
Their dark impenetrable wood,
Each stepping where his comrade stood
The instant that he fell.
No thought was there of dastard flight:
Link'd in the serried phalanx tight,
Groom fought like noble, squire like knight,
As fearlessly and well;
Till utter darkness closed her wing
O'er their thin host and wounded King.
Then skilful Surrey's sage commands

Led back from strife his shattered bands;
  And from the charge they drew,
As mountain-waves, from wasted lands,
  Sweep back to ocean blue.
Then did their loss his foemen know;
Their King, their lords, their mightiest low,
They melted from the field as snow,
When streams are swoln and south winds blow
  Dissolves in silent dew.

. . . .

Still from the sire the son shall hear
Of the stern fight and carnage drear
  Of Flodden's fatal field,
Where shiver'd was fair Scotland's spear,
  And broken was her shield!

. . . . . .

And well in death his trusty brand,
Firm clench'd within his manly hand
  Beseem'd the Monarch slain."

Chapter XX

After Flodden

SO deeply did the tragic result of Flodden touch the hearts of the Scottish people that no Scot could for many a long day hear it mentioned without a heart-thrill.

Many are the songs written about it, the most famous perhaps, being the "Flowers of the Forest," written two centuries later, though partly founded upon an older and almost forgotten song.

THE FLOWERS OF THE FOREST

I've heard them lilting, at our ewe-milking,
  Lasses a' lilting, before dawn o' day;
But now they are moaning on ilka green loaning [1]
  The Flowers of the Forest are a' wede away.

At bughts, in the morning, nae blythe lads are scorning; [2]
  The lasses are lonely, and dowie, and wae;
Wae daffing,[3] nae gabbing,[4] but sighing and sabbing;
  Ilk ane lifts her leglin,[5] and hies her away.

In hair'st, at the shearing, nae youths now are jeering,
  The bandsters [6] are runkled,[7] and lyart [8] or gray;
At fair, or at preaching, nae wooing, nae fleeching; [9]
  The Flowers of the Forest are a' wede away.

[1] a broad grassy lane used as milking-ground.
[2] rallying. [3] joking. [4] chatting. [5] milking-pail.
[6] sheaf-binders. [7] wrinkled. [8] inclining to grey. [9] coaxing.

At e'en, in the gloaming, nae younkers are roaming
  'Bout stacks with the lasses at bogle to play;
But ilk maid sits dreary, lamenting her deary—
  The Flowers of the Forest are a' wede away.

Dool and wae for the order, sent our lads to the Border!
  The English, for ance, by guile wan the day:
The Flowers of the Forest, that fought aye the foremost,
  The prime of our land, are cauld in the clay.

We'll hear nae mair lilting at the ewe-milking;
  Women and bairns are heartless and wae:
Sighing and moaning on ilka green loaning—
  The Flowers of the Forest are a' wede away.

JEAN ELLIOT (1727-1805).

The following poem also gives eloquent and touching expression to the deep gloom which descended upon the Border after the fatal battle, and tells of the despair felt in almost every Ettrick home:—

SELKIRK AFTER FLODDEN

(A WIDOW'S DIRGE, OCTOBER 1513)

IT'S but a month the morn
  Sin' a' was peace and plenty;
Oor hairst was halflins shorn,
  Eident men and lasses denty.
But noo it's a' distress—
  Never mair a merry meetin';
For half the bairns are faitherless,
  And a' the women greetin'.
      O Flodden Field!

Miles and miles round Selkirk toun,
  Where forest flow'rs are fairest,
Ilka lassie's stricken doun,
  Wi' the fate that fa's the sairest.
A' the lads they used to meet
  By Ettrick braes or Yarrow
Lyin' thrammelt head and feet
  In Brankstone's deadly barrow!
    O Flodden Field!

Frae every cleuch and clan
  The best o' the braid Border
Rose like a single man
  To meet the royal order.
Oor Burgh toun itsel'
  Sent its seventy doun the glen;
Ask Fletcher [1] how they fell,
  Bravely fechtin', ane to ten!
    O Flodden Field!

Round about their gallant king,
  For country and for croun,
Stude the dauntless Border ring,
  Till the last was hackit doun.
I blame na what has been—
  They maun fa' that canna flee—
But oh, to see what I hae seen,
  To see what now I see!
    O Flodden Field!

[1] This was the man who brought an English flag back to Selkirk from Flodden. Four brothers of that name are said to have perished in the battle.

The souters a' fu' croose,
  O'er their leather and their lingle,
Wi' their shoon in ilka hoose,
  Sat contentit round the ingle.
Noo there's naething left but dool,—
  Never mair their work will cheer them;
In Flodden's bluidy pool
  They'll neither walt nor wear them!
      O Flodden Field!

Whar the weavers used to meet,
  In ilka bieldy corner,
Noo there's nane in a' the street,
  Savin' here and there a mourner,
Walkin' lonely as a wraith,
  Or if she meet anither,
Just a word below their braith
  O' some slauchtered son or brither!
      O Flodden Field!

There stands the gudeman's loom
  That used tae gang sae cheerie,
Untentit noo, and toom,
  Makin' a' the hoose sae eerie,
Till the sicht I canna dree;
  For the shuttles lyin' dumb
Speak the loudlier to me
  O' him that wunna come.
      O Flodden Field!

Sae at nicht I cover't o'er,
  Just to haud it frae my een,

But I haena yet the pow'r
  To forget what it has been;
And I listen through the hoose
  For the chappin o' the lay,
Till the scrapin' o' a moose
  Tak's my very braith away.
    O Flodden Field!

Then I turn to sister Jean,
  And my airms aboot her twine,
And I kiss her sleepless een,
  For her heart's as sair as mine,—
A heart ance fu' o' fun,
  And hands that ne'er were idle,
Wi' a' her cleedin' spun
  Against her Jamie's bridal.
    O Flodden Field!

Noo we've naether hands nor hairt—
  In oor grief the wark's forgotten,
Though it's wantit every airt,
  And the craps are lyin' rotten.
War's awsome blast's gane bye,
  And left a land forlorn;
In daith's dool hairst they lie,
  The shearers and the shorn.
    O Flodden Field.

Wi' winter creepin' near us,
  When the nichts are drear and lang,
Nane to help us, nane to hear us,
  On the weary gate we gang!

Lord o' the quick an' deed,
  Sin' oor ain we canna see,
In mercy mak gude speed,
  And bring us whar they be,
    Far, far, frae Flodden Field!

"J. B. Selkirk" (James B. Brown).

By permission of W. Cuthbertson, Esq.

Another lyric, relating to the fatal battle of Flodden, refers to the gallantry of the Souters, or shoemakers of Selkirk, who, to the number of eighty, and headed by their town-clerk, joined the army as it entered England. They distinguished themselves greatly, and few returned. The "yellow and green" are the liveries of the house of Home, taxed by some with being the cause of the defeat.

THE SOUTERS OF SELKIRK

Up wi' the Souters of Selkirk,
  And doun wi' the Earl of Home;
And up wi' a' the braw lads
  That sew the single-soled shoon.

Fye upon yellow and yellow,
  And fye upon yellow and green,
But up wi' the true blue and scarlet,
  And up wi' the single-soled sheen.

Up wi' the Souters of Selkirk,
  For they are baith trusty and leal;
And up wi' the men o' the Forest,
  And doun wi' the Merse to the deil.

In Aytoun's "Lays of the Scottish Cavaliers," the following well-known poem tells how the news of the disaster at Flodden Field was received in Edinburgh:—

EDINBURGH AFTER FLODDEN

I

News of battle! news of battle!
Hark! 'tis ringing down the street:
And the archways and the pavement
Bear the clang of hurrying feet.
News of battle! Who hath brought it?
News of triumph! Who should bring
Tidings from our noble army,
Greetings from our gallant King?
All last night we watched the beacons
Blazing on the hills afar,
Each one bearing, as it kindled,
Message of the opened war.
All night long the northern streamers
Shot across the trembling sky:
Fearful lights that never beckon
Save when kings or heroes die.

II

News of battle! Who hath brought it?
All are thronging to the gate;
"Warder—warder! open quickly!
Man—is this a time to wait?"
And the heavy gates are opened;
Then a murmur long and loud,

And a cry of fear and wonder
Bursts from out the bending crowd.
For they see in battered harness
Only one hard-stricken man ;
And his weary steed is wounded,
And his cheek is pale and wan.
Spearless hangs a bloody banner
In his weak and drooping hand—
God ! can that be Randolph Murray,
Captain of the city band ?

III

Round him crush the people, crying,
" Tell us all—oh, tell us true !
Where are they who went to battle,
Randolph Murray, sworn to you ?
Where are they, our brothers—children ?
Have they met the English foe ?
Why art thou alone, unfollowed ?
Is it weal, or is it woe ? "
Like a corpse the grisly warrior
Looks from out his helm of steel ;
But no word he speaks in answer—
Only with his armèd heel
Chides his weary steed, and onward
Up the city streets they ride ;
Fathers, sisters, mothers, children,
Shrieking, praying by his side.
" By the God that made thee, Randolph !
Tell us what mischance hath come."
Then he lifts his riven banner,
And the asker's voice is dumb.

"Tell us all—oh, tell us true!"

IV

The elders of the city
Have met within their hall—
The men whom good King James had charged
To watch the tower and wall.
" Your hands are weak with age," he said,
" Your hearts are stout and true ;
So bide ye in the maiden town,
While others fight for you.
My trumpet from the Border-side
Shall send a blast so clear,
That all who wait within the gate
That stirring sound may hear.
Or, if it be the will of Heaven
That back I never come,
And if, instead of Scottish shout,
Ye hear the English drum,
Then let the warning bells ring out,
Then gird you to the fray,
Then man the walls like burghers stout,
And fight while fight you may.
'Twere better that in fiery flame
The roofs should thunder down,
Than that the foot of foreign foe
Should trample in the town ! "

V

Then in came Randolph Murray,
His step was slow and weak,
And, as he doffed his dinted helm.
The tears ran down his cheek :
They fell upon his corslet
And on his mailèd hand,

As he gazed around him wistfully,
Leaning sorely on his brand.
And none who then beheld him
But straight were smote with fear,
For a bolder and a sterner man
Had never couched a spear.
They knew so sad a messenger
Some ghastly news must bring;
And all of them were fathers,
And their sons were with the King.

VI

And up then rose the Provost—
A brave old man was he,
Of ancient name, and knightly fame,
And chivalrous degree.
He ruled our city like a Lord
Who brooked no equal here,
And ever for the townsmen's rights
Stood up 'gainst prince and peer.
And he had seen the Scottish host
March from the Borough muir,
With music-storm and clamorous shout,
And all the din that thunders out
When youth's of victory sure.
But yet a dearer thought had he;—
For, with a father's pride,
He saw his last remaining son
Go forth by Randolph's side,
With casque on head and spur on heel,
All keen to do and dare;
And proudly did that gallant boy
Dunedin's banner bear.

Oh! woeful now was the old man's look,
And he spake right heavily—
" Now, Randolph, tell thy tidings,
However sharp they be!
Woe is written on thy visage,
Death is looking from thy face;
Speak! though it be of overthrow—
It cannot be disgrace!"

VII

Right bitter was the agony
That wrung that soldier proud;
Thrice did he strive to answer,
And thrice he groaned aloud.
Then he gave the riven banner
To the old man's shaking hand,
Saying—" That is all I bring ye
From the bravest of the land!
Ay! ye may look upon it—
It was guarded well and long,
By your brothers and your children,
By the valiant and the strong.
One by one they fell around it,
As the archers laid them low,
Grimly dying, still unconquered,
With their faces to the foe.
Ay! ye may well look upon it—
There is more than honour there,
Else, be sure, I had not brought it
From the field of dark despair.
Never yet was royal banner
Steeped in such a costly dye;

It hath lain upon a bosom
Where no other shroud shall lie.
Sirs! I charge you, keep it holy;
Keep it as a sacred thing,
For the stain ye see upon it
Was the life-blood of your King!"

VIII

Woe and woe and lamentation!
What a piteous cry was there!
Widows, maidens, mothers, children,
Shrieking, sobbing in despair!
Through the streets the death-word rushes,
Spreading terror, sweeping on.
"Jesu Christ! our King has fallen—
O Great God, King James is gone!
Holy mother Mary, shield us,
Thou who erst did lose thy Son!
O the blackest day for Scotland
That she ever knew before!
O our King—the good, the noble,
Shall we see him never more?
Woe to us, and woe to Scotland!
O our sons, our sons and men!
Surely some have 'scaped the Southron,
Surely some will come again!"

Randolph Murray describes how the monarch lies dead on the field with his nobles round him.

"All so thick they lay together,
When the stars lit up the sky,
That I knew not who were stricken,
Or who yet remained to die."

A hollow knell is rung and the miserere is sung, and all is terror and disorder until the Provost rouses them.

"If our King be taken from us,
We are left to guard his son.

. . . .

Up! and haste ye through the city,
Stir the burghers stout and true!
Gather all our scattered people,
Fling the banner out once more—
Randolph Murray! do thou bear it,
As it erst was borne before:
Never Scottish heart will leave it,
When they see their monarch's gore!"

Chapter XXI

Graeme and Bewick

GOOD Lord Graeme and Sir Robert Bewick were friends. They met one day in Carlisle, and went arm in arm to the wine, and, as was too oft the custom of these days, they stayed and drank till they were both merry. Good Lord Graeme took up the cup. " Sir Robert, and here's to thee ! " he said, " and here's to our two sons at home, for they like us best in our own country."

" O were your son a lad like mine," answered Bewick, boastfully, " and learnt some books that he could read, they might be two brothers in arms, and lord it over the Borderside.

> 'But your son's a lad, and he's but bad,
> And billie [1] to my son he cannot be.'

You sent him to school, and he would not learn ; you bought him books, and he would not read ! "

Lord Graeme called angrily for the reckoning. " My blessing shall he never earn," said he, " till I see how his arm can defend his head." He threw down a crown, and went to the stable, took his horse, and rode home. " Welcome, my old father," said his son, Christie Graeme, " but where were ye so long from home ? " " I have been at Carlisle town, and a shamed man I am by thee,"

[1] Comrade, or brother-in-arms.

answered his father with a black look; "I have been at Carlisle town, where Sir Robert Bewick met me. He says you are but a bad, wild youth, and can never be billie to his boy. I sent you to the school, and you would not learn. I bought you books, and you would not read; therefore you shall never have my blessing till I see you save your head in fight with young Bewick." "Now God forbid, my old father, that ever such a thing should be! Billie Bewick was my master, and I his scholar, in spite of the pains he wasted in teaching me." "O hold thy tongue, thou foolish lad! If thou dost not soon end this quarrel, there's my glove, I'll fight with thee myself."

Then Christie Graeme stooped low. "Father, put on your glove again, the wind has blown it from your hand."

"What's that, thou sayst, thou limmer loon?
How darest thou stand to speak to me?
If thou do not end this quarrel soon,
There's my right hand, thou'lt fight with me!"

Then went Christie to his chamber, to consider what should happen. Should he fight with his own father, or with his brother-in-arms, Bewick?

"If I should kill my billie dear,
God's blessing I shall never win;
But if I strike at my auld father,
I think 'twould be a mortal sin.
But if I kill my billie dear
It is God's will, so let it be;
But I make a vow, ere I go from home,
That I shall be the next man's die."

He put a good old jack or quilted doublet on his back, and on his head he put a cap of steel, and well did he become them with his sword and buckler by his side!

Now young Bewick had taken his father's sword under

his arm, and walked about his father's close. He looked between himself and the sun, to see some approaching object, and was aware of a man in bright armour, riding that way most hastily.

> "O who is yon, that comes this way,
> So hastily that hither came?
> I think it be my brother dear,
> I think it be young Christie Graeme.
> Your welcome here, my billie dear,
> And thrice you're welcome unto me."

Christie explained that he was come to fight, that his father had been to Carlisle, and had met with the elder Bewick. He retailed what had passed, "and so I'll never earn my father's blessing, till he sees how my arm can guard my head in fight against thee."

> "O God forbid, my billie dear,
> That ever such a thing should be!
> We'll take three men on either side,
> And see if we can our fathers agree."

Christie shook his head. He knew that it was useless. "O hold thy tongue, billie Bewick. If thou'rt a man, as I'm sure thou art, come over the dyke and fight with me."

"But I have no harness, billie, as I see you have."

"As little harness as is on your back shall be on mine."

With that Christie threw off his coat of mail and cap of steel, stuck his spear into the ground, and tied his horse up to a tree. Bewick threw off his cloak, and cast aside his psalter book. He laid his hand upon the dyke, and vaulted over. The two fought for two long hours. The sweat dropped fast from them both, but not a drop of blood could be seen to satisfy the requirements of honour. At last Graeme hit Bewick under the left breast, and he fell to the ground wounded mortally.

"Rise up, rise up, now, billie dear,
Arise and speak three words to me!
Whether thou's gotten thy deadly wound,
Or if God and good leeching[1] may succour thee?"

Bewick groaned. "Get to horse, billie Graeme, and get thee hence speedily. Get thee out of this country—that none may know who has done this." "O have I slain thee, billie Bewick? But I made a vow, ere I came from home, that I would be the next man to die!" Thereupon he pitched his sword hilt downwards into a mole-hill, took a run of some three and twenty feet, and on his own sword's point he fell to the ground dead.

Then up came Sir Robert Bewick. "Rise up, my son," he said, "for I think you have got the victory."

"O hold your tongue, my father dear. Let me be spared your prideful talking. You might have drunken your wine in peace, and let me and my billie be! Go dig a grave, both wide and deep, and a grave to hold us both; but lay Christie Graeme on the sunny side, for full sure I know that the victory was to him."

"Alas," cried old Bewick, "I've lost the liveliest lad that ever was born unto my name." "Alas," quoth good Lord Graeme, "my loss is the greater.

'I've lost my hopes, I've lost my joy,
I've lost the key, but and the lock;
I durst have ridden the world around,
Had Christie Graeme been at my back!'"

[1] Doctoring.

Chapter XXII

The Song of the Outlaw Murray

> "Word is gone to our noble king,
> In Edinburgh where that he lay,
> That there was an Outlaw in Ettrick Forest
> Counted him nought, nor all his Court so gay."

THE King mentioned in the ballad is supposed to have been either James IV. or James V. This places the date somewhere in the early part of the sixteenth century.

The Outlaw Murray and his lady kept royal state in Ettrick Forest. Here he lived with five hundred men, all gaily clad in livery of Lincoln green. His castle, built of lime and stone, stood fair and pleasantly in the midst of the Forest, surrounded by pine trees under which wandered many a hart and hind, many a doe and roe and other wild creatures. In the forefront of the castle stood two unicorns, with the picture of a knight and lady with green holly above their brows.

The King in Edinburgh heard of all this royal state and that the Outlaw in Ettrick Forest cared nought for the King of Scotland and his court.

"I make a vow," said the King, "that either I shall be King of Ettrick Forest, or the Outlaw shall be King of Scotland."

Then up spoke Lord Hamilton to the noble King, "my sovereign prince, take counsel of your nobles and of me.

I counsel ye to send to the fine Outlaw and see if he will come and be your man and hold the Forest in fee from you. If he refuse, we will conquer both him and his lands, throw his castle down, and make a widow of his gay lady."

Then the King called to him James Boyd, son of the Earl of Arran, and when Boyd came and knelt before him, "Welcome, James Boyd," said the noble King; "you must go for me to Ettrick Forest where bides yonder Outlaw, ask him of whom he holds his lands, and who is his master, and desire him to come and be my man, and hold the Forest free from me. I will give him safe warrant to and from Edinburgh, and if he refuse we will conquer him and his lands, and throw down his castle, and make a widow of his gay lady; and hang his merry men pair by pair wherever we see them."

James Boyd took leave of the King and went blithely on his way, until he came to the fair Ettrick Forest, the first view of which he got coming down Birkendale Brae. He saw the doe and roe, the hart and hind and wild beasts in plenty, and heard blows ringing boldly, and arrows whizzing near by him.

He saw, too, the fair castle, the like of which he had never seen before, with the two gay unicorns on the forefront, and the picture of the knight and lady with the green holly above their brow.

Then he spied the five hundred men, all clad in livery of Lincoln green, and shooting with their bows on Newark Lee. In the midst of them was a knight armed from head to foot, mounted on a milk-white steed, with bended bow, all fine to look upon; whom Boyd knew at once to be the Outlaw himself.

"God save thee, brave Outlaw Murray, thy lady, and all thy chivalry!"

"Marry, thou art welcome, gentleman; thou seemst to be a King's messenger."

"The King of Scotland sent me here, good Outlaw, to know of whom you hold your lands, and who is your master."

"These lands are *mine*. I know no King in Christendom. I won this Forest from the English when neither the King nor his knights were there to see."

"The King desires that you come to Edinburgh, and hold the Forest then of him. If you refuse, he will conquer your lands and you, and he has vowed to throw down your castle, make a widow of your gay lady, and hang your knights pair by pair wherever he finds them."

"Ay, by my troth! I should indeed be far behind. Before the King should get my fair native land, many of his nobles would be cold, and their ladies right weary."

Then spoke the lady of the Outlaw, fair of face. "That an Outlaw should come before the King without my consent makes me fear much that there is treason. Bid him be good to his lords at home, for my lord shall ne'er see Edinburgh."

James Boyd took leave of the bold Outlaw and went back to Edinburgh, and when he came to the King, knelt lowly on his knee.

"Welcome, James Boyd," said the noble King, "of whom is Ettrick Forest held?"

"Ettrick Forest is the fairest forest that ever man saw. There are doe and roe and hart and hind and wild beasts in plenty; there's a fine castle of lime and stone standing there pleasantly, and in the forefront of the castle two unicorns all fine to see, with a picture of a knight and a lady, and the green holly above their brows. There the Outlaw keeps a royal company—five hundred merry men, all gaily clad in Lincoln green, and the Outlaw and his lady in purple. Surely they live right royally. He says that the forest is his own, that he won it from the English, and that as he won it, so will he keep it against all the Kings in Christendom."

"Go warn me Perthshire and Angus," cried the King "go warn Fife up and down and the three Lothians, and harness my own horse, for I will myself to Ettrick Forest."

When the Outlaw heard that the King was coming to his country to conquer him and his lands:

"I make a vow," said he. "I make a vow, and that truly, that the King's coming shall be a dear one."

Then he called messengers and sent them in haste hither and thither.

"One of you go to Halliday, Laird of Corehead, my sister's son. Tell him to come quickly to my aid, for that the King comes to Ettrick Forest, and we shall all be landless."

"What news? What news, man, from thy master?" said Halliday.

"No news thou carest to hear; I come seeking your aid; the King is his mortal enemy."

"By my troth, I am sorry for that; if Murray lose fair Ettrick Forest, the King will take Moffatdale from me. I'll meet him with five hundred men, and more if need be, and before he gets to Ettrick Forest, we will all die on Newark Lee."

Another messenger went from the Outlaw to Andrew Murray of Cockpool, his dear cousin, to desire him to come and help him with all the power he could get together.

"It is hard," said Andrew Murray, "very hard to go against a crowned King and put my lands in jeopardy; but if I come not by day I shall be there at night."

A messenger went also to Sir James Murray of Traquair.

"What news? What news, man, from your master to me?" said James Murray.

"What need I tell? Well ye know that the King is his mortal enemy and that he is coming to Ettrick Forest to make ye all landless men."

"By my troth," said James Murray, "with yonder Outlaw will I live and die; the King has long ago given away my lands, so matters can be no worse for me."

So the King came on with five thousand men through Caddon Ford. They saw the dark forest before them and thought it awesome to look upon, and Lord Hamilton begged that the King should take counsel of his nobles and should desire the Outlaw to meet him at Permanscore with four of his company and that the King should go there also accompanied by five Earls. "If he refuse to do that, we'll conquer both him and his lands; there shall never a Murray after him hold lands free in Ettrick Forest."

The Laird of Buckscleuth, a man stalwart and stern, thought it beneath the state and dignity of a King to go and meet an Outlaw. "The man that lives in yonder forest, lives by robbery and felony! wherefore, ride on, my liege; we will follow thee with fire and sword; or if your courtier lords fall back, our Borderers will make the onset."

But the King spoke forth, casting a wily glance around. "Thou mayest hold *thy* tongue, Sir Walter Scott, nor speak more of robbery and felony, for if every honest man had his own cattle thy clan would be a poor one."

The King then called to him a gentleman, a royal banner-bearer, James Hoppringle of Torsonse by name, who came and knelt before him. "Welcome, James Pringle of Torsonse, ye must take a message for me; go to yonder Outlaw Murray, where he bideth so boldly; bid him meet me at Permanscore with four of his company, I myself will come to him with five Earls. If he refuse, bid him look for no favour from me. There shall never a Murray after him have free land in Ettrick Forest."

So James Pringle came before the Outlaw. "Welcome James Pringle of Torsonse! What message bringst thou from the King to me?"

"He bids ye meet him at Permanscore, with four of your company, and he will go there himself with no more than five Earls. If you refuse, he will cast down your bonny castle, make a widow of your gay lady, and loose on you the bloodhound Borderers to harry you with fire and sword. Never shall a Murray after you hold free land in Ettrick Forest."

"It goes hard with me," said the Outlaw; "judge if it go not very hard. I mind not the losing of myself, but when I think of my offspring after me, my merry men's lives, my widow's tears, that is the pang that pinches me. Yonder castle will be right dreary when I am laid in bloody earth. Auld Halliday, young Halliday, ye two shall go with me, with Andrew and James Murray."

When they came before the King they fell on their knees. "Mercy, mercy, noble King, for His sake who died on the Cross."

"Such mercy shall ye have; ye shall be hanged on the gallows."

"May God forbid, and may your mercy be better than that, else, when ye come to the port of Edinburgh, ye shall be thinly guarded. These lands of fair Ettrick Forest I won from the Southrons, and as I won them so will I keep them, against all the Kings in Christendom."

The nobles round the King thought it a pity that he should die.

"Grant me mercy, sovereign prince, and extend me favour. If thou wilt make me Sheriff of Ettrick Forest, and my offspring after me, I will give thee the keys of my castle, and the blessing of my gay lady."

"If thou wilt give me thy castle keys and the blessing of thy gay lady, I'll make thee Sheriff of Ettrick Forest as long as the trees grow upward, and never shalt thou forfeit it, if thou be not a traitor to the King."

"But Prince, what shall become of my men? When I go back they will call me traitor. I had rather lose both life and land than be rebuked by my merry-men."

"I will pardon them all if they amend their lives. Name thy lands where they lie, and I will render them back to thee."

"Philiphaugh and Lewinhope are mine by right, Newark, Foulshiells and Tinnies I won by my bow and arrow. I have farms at Newark Lee and Hangingshaw which are mine by birth, and I have many farms in the Forest whose names I do not know." Thereupon he gave the King the key of his castle, with the blessing of his fair lady, and the King made him Sheriff of Ettrick Forest for as long as the trees should grow upward, never to be forfeited while he and his descendants remained faithful to the King. Much of this land belongs to Murray's heirs, even to this day.

> "Wha ever heard in, in ony times,
> Sicken an outlaw in his degré,
> Sic favour got befor a King,
> As did the Outlaw Murray or the Foreste free?"

Chapter XXIII

Johnie Armstrong

"When Johnie came before the King,
With all his men so brave to see,
The King he moved his bonnet to him;
He knew he was a King as well as he."

IN 1529 James V. visited the Border country to execute justice on the wild freebooters.

Of these the chief was Johnie Armstrong of Gilnockie, who levied blackmail for many miles round his residence at the Hollows, and spread the terror of his name as far as Newcastle. Acting on the evil counsel of false friends, Johnie presented himself before the King in all the pomp of Border chivalry.

According to the old ballad the King wrote with his own hand a loving letter to Johnie Armstrong, Laird of Gilnockie, bidding him come and speak with him speedily. Whereupon the Elliots and Armstrongs convened a meeting, to which they came in gallant company, and decided to ride out to meet the King and bring him to Gilnockie.

"Make ready rabbits and capon and venison in plenty," said Johnie, and we'll welcome home our royal King to dine at Gilnockie."

So they ran out their horses on Langholm Down, and broke their spears, and the ladies, looking from their high windows, cried "God send our men safe home again."

When Johnie came before the King with all his brave fellows, the King took off his bonnet to him as to an equal.

"My name is Johnie Armstrong," said the freebooter, "your subject, my liege; let me find grace for my loyal men and me."

But the King cried, "Away with thee, thou traitor, out of my sight! Never have I granted a traitor's life, nor will I now begin with thee!"

"Grant me my life, my King, and I will give thee a bonnie gift—four-and-twenty milk-white steeds, newly foaled—I'll give thee four-and-twenty milk-white steeds that prance and neigh at a spear, and as much English gold as four of their broad backs are able to bear."

"Away with thee, thou traitor, out of my sight! Never have I granted a traitor's life, nor will I now begin with thee!"

"Grant me my life, my King, and I will give thee a bonnie gift—four-and-twenty mills that are working all the year round for me—four-and-twenty mills that shall go for thee all the year round, and as much good red wheat as all their happers are able to bear."

"Away with thee, thou traitor, out of my sight! Never have I granted a traitor's life, nor will I now begin with thee!"

"Grant me my life, my King, and I will give thee a great gift—four-and-twenty sisters' sons shall fight for thee though all should flee."

"Away with thee, thou traitor, out of my sight! Never have I granted a traitor's life, nor will I now begin with thee!"

"Grant me my life, my King, and I will give thee a brave gift. All between here and Newcastle town shall pay thee yearly rent."

"Away with thee, thou traitor, out of my sight! Never have I granted a traitor's life, nor will I now begin with thee!"

"Ye lie, calling me traitor; ye lie now, King, although ye be King and Prince. Well dare I say it, that all my life I have loved naught but honesty, a fleet horse, a fair woman, and two bonny dogs to kill a deer; yet had I lived for another hundred years, England should have still found me meal and malt and plenty of beef and mutton. Never would a Scot's wife have been able to say that I robbed her of aught. But surely it is great folly to seek for hot water beneath cold ice. I have asked grace of a graceless King, but there is none for me and my men. But had I known before I came how unkind thou wouldst prove to me, I would have kept the Border-side in spite of thee and thy nobles. How glad would be England's King if he but knew that I was taken, for once I slew his sister's son and broke a tree over his breast-bone."

Now Johnie had a girdle round his waist embroidered and spangled with burning gold, very beautiful to look upon, and from his hat hung down nine tassels, each worth three hundred pounds. "What wants that knave that a King should have, but the sword of honour and the crown?" cried the King.

"Where did ye get those tassels, Johnie, that shine so bravely above your brow?"

"I got them fighting in the field where thou darest not be," replied Johnie. "And had I now my horse and good harness, and were I riding as I am used to do, this meeting between us should have been told these hundred years. God be with thee, my brother Christy, long shalt thou live Laird of Mangertown on the Border-side ere thou see thy brother ride by again. God be with *thee*, my son

Christy, where thou sitst on thy nurse's knee; thou'lt ne'er be a better man than thy father, though thou live a hundred years. Farewell, bonnie Hall of Gilnockie, standing strong on Eskside; if I had lived but seven more years, I would have gilded thee round about."

Then Johnie Armstrong was slain by the King's orders at Carlinrigg with all his gallant company, and Scotland's heart was sad to see the death of so many brave men, who had saved their country from the Englishmen. None were so brave as they, and while Johnie lived on the Border-side no Englishman durst come near his stronghold.

Chapter XXIV

The Lament of the Border Widow

HOW King James V. of Scotland, in 1529, set forth to strike terror into the Border freebooters, has been already told in the account of Johnie Armstrong. A less celebrated moss-trooper, Cockburne of Henderland, was hanged by the pitiless King over the gate of his own tower. The wife of Cockburne loved him most dearly, and when she found the King would show no mercy, fled away to the rocks behind the castle whilst the cruel sentence was carried out. She sat by a roaring torrent of the Henderland burn, the noise of which in her ears drowned the savage shouts of the King's soldiers. The beautiful song which describes the grief of this loving woman is one of the gems of ancient poetry, and is here printed entire.

THE LAMENT OF THE BORDER WIDOW

My love he built me a bonny bower,
And clad it a' wi' lilye flower,
A brawer bower ye ne'er did see,
Than my true love he built for me.

There came a man by middle day,
He spied his sport, and went away;

And brought the King that very night,
Who brake my bower, and slew my knight.

He slew my knight to me sae dear;
He slew my knight, and took his gear;
My servants all for life did flee,
And left me in extremitie.

I sew'd his sheet, making my moan;
I watch'd the corpse, myself alone;
I watch'd his body, night and day;
No living creature came that way.

I took his body on my back,
And whiles I gaed, and whiles I sat;
I digg'd a grave, and laid him in,
And happ'd him with the sod sae green.

But think na ye my heart was sair,
When I laid the moul' on his yellow hair;
O think na ye my heart was wae,
When I turn'd about, away to gae?

Nae living man I'll love again,
Since that my lovely knight was slain,
Wi' ae lock of his yellow hair,
I'll chain my heart for evermair.

"I sew'd his sheet, making my moan;
I watch'd the corpse, myself alone."

Chapter XXV

The Raid of the Kers

THE spirited ballad that describes this raid is quite modern, since it was written by Hogg, "the Ettrick Shepherd," in 1830. But the rash raid it describes took place in 1549. The Kers were an important Border family, the leaders of whom afterwards became Earls of Roxburgh. Sir Andrew Ker was warden of the Border at the time of the raid, but he proved that it took place without his consent. The Kers were all left-handed men, and puzzled their enemies by their left-handed swordsmanship. Even to-day in some parts of the borders a left-handed man is called "Ker-handed."

On a fine September evening Tam Ker rode out, with fifty in his company. They were armed for a fight and their swords were keen; they rode by the Maiden Crags and down the Osway burn, going carefully till the daylight closed, for they were soon in Northumberland. Their bold plan was to get down the valley of the Coquet even as far as Rothbury where Withrington, the English warden, kept a magnificent herd of cattle. They had one castle to pass, that of Biddleston, which had been held by the Selby family since the reign of Henry III., and still belongs to them to this day. Biddleston Castle guarded the Allanton or Alwinton ford, where the Alwin stream enters the Coquet. So they sent the reckless Mark Ker first, to scout along by the ford, and told him to set up marks on the cairns to show his progress. Having nothing else to mark with, he tore the shirt off his back, and left strips of it on the cairns. At the ford a sentry challenged him, and he answered that he had a message for Withrington. The sentry demanded his sealed warrant, and the Scot drew his sword. They fought bravely and long before the Englishman was killed, and the Scot marvelled that a common soldier should so withstand him, for he was the best swordsman of his race. On he galloped, on and on, till he met a comely maiden, and addressing her he tried to imitate the Northumberland speech, saying that he had lost his way. She told him at once that she knew he was a Scot, but so also was she. She had been taken captive, but word had came by an English spy that the Kers were out upon a raid, and while the English had set a hundred soldiers to guard their cattle she had slipped away to warn the Scots and to return with them. Being a gallant after the manner of that day, he sprang from his horse, kissed her, and invited her to mount his saddle even if he had to run beside till he could capture another steed. But an English soldier came up and warned him roughly off the road. Mark Ker had been brought up to answer rough words with rougher blows; out leapt his sword, and he cut the rude words short by slashing the man's head off. Then he disguised the maid in the dead man's clothes, and they retraced their steps that he might warn his companions. They very soon came upon them, and all together hid in the lowest dell of the Larbottle burn while they made their plans. Tam Ker, with twenty of the men, was to draw off the English, while Mark with thirty others slipped round and drove off the cattle unperceived. This was done, and till after midnight, Tam, aided by the darkness and by the difficulties of the wild locality, held the English at bay.

Then he heard the bugle signal, and knew that Mark was well on the road with the beasts, and that he must follow quickly. But Withrington also guessed what the signal meant, and pursued with all the speed he knew. Mark had not long crossed the ford at Biddleston before the English were on him. First Mark and Withrington fought in single combat, hand to hand, all their men watching eagerly; it was still very dark, but the clash of sword against sword lit the air with sparks. Withrington was badly wounded, but Mark was killed. With desperate shouts the Scots fell upon the English; then up came Tam and his men from behind to help the Scots, but the Captain of Biddleston had also been awakened, and galloped down with his men to aid the English. Tam smote his head off with his sword, but the horse galloped on with his headless body right into the ranks of the Scots. They thought it must be a demon and began to scatter in full flight to the Border. Tam was slain, trying to follow them, and his men, seeing that they had work enough to gallop for their lives, slew the cattle they could no longer hope to steal. On and on the hard-pressed remnant spurred their weary horses. It was daylight now, and the English along the road shot arrows at them as they galloped past. Out of fifty-one hardy, healthy Kers who had started forth in the raid, only seventeen, weary and wounded, saw their homes again.

And back in the south country, the comely Scottish maiden lay dead across the breast of the gallant Mark, their hearts' blood mingling in a common stream. Small wonder that a Scot should make a ballad of the story and that Borderers should sing it even to this day.

Chapter XXVI

Merrie Carlisle

THE city of Carlisle stands in the midst of a beautiful and fertile district with pleasant but not too steep hills around. In the old days an easy water-supply was a first essential, and at Carlisle three rivers meet, the Caldew and the Petterill running here into the broad stream of the Eden. These three rivers almost enclose the ground upon which the city is built, so that it is most probable that there was an ancient British settlement upon so advantageous a site, before the Roman invasion. Our earliest record, however, goes back no further than Roman days, and it is certain there was then a Roman city here called *Luguvallium* (the trench of the legion). Even to-day, when new gas-pipes are being laid in the ground, it is by no means rare to dig up Roman relics. The long Roman name became gradually corrupted into "Luel," or "Liel," and the Britons added their word "Caer," which means a city, hence "Caer-luel"—an earlier form of the modern Carlisle. The Roman city stood, as might be expected, by the great Roman wall, guarding the spot where the wall crossed the river Eden. And visitors may see to-day that the centre of Carlisle consists of a market-place with two main streets leading therefrom, the usual plan in cities of Roman origin.

Carlisle was destined to have a stormy history. Draw

a line from the Solway eastward, straight through Carlisle, and it will be seen that here the mainland of Britain is about at its narrowest, hardly so much as seventy miles wide, as the crow flies. Note, too, that the wild hills of the Pennines and the Cheviots fill in most of this narrow district, and that the mainland of Scotland strikes sharply off to the west. It is plain from these facts that Carlisle commands the main road between Scotland and England, and they provide the reason why at the present day seven different railways, most of them important ones, run their trains into Carlisle station. The very same reason was responsible for the fact that in the good old times no English town was more often burnt down by enemies than "Merrie Carlisle."

Even in Roman days, during the reign of Nero, Carlisle was burnt down at least once by the wild Picts, who were brave enough to venture against the well-armed troops of Rome. After the Romans left Britain this town was one of the strongholds of King Arthur; to be sure, nothing very definite is known about this romantic king, but the old ballads tell us that he was victorious over Gauls, Dacians, Spaniards, and Romans. This sounds very unlikely to those who do not realise that when Rome called home her best men for her own defence she may have left behind many rough soldiers, of various nations, to guard the wall. Although we know nothing about King Arthur save what is vague and legendary, we do know that the Roman legions were recruited from all the provinces of the empire. Cumberland had many connexions with King Arthur; within twenty miles of Carlisle, near Penrith, is a big round hill called "King Arthur's Table"; while nearer still, on the Penrith and Carlisle road, is shown the spot where stood Tearne-Wadling Lake and Castle, where King

Arthur was bewitched and taken prisoner by the "foul, discourteous knight," only to be released provided one of his men would consent to marry the hideous lady with hair like serpents! When at last Sir Gawaine married this hag for his King's sake, she, of course, changed at once into a beautiful young woman! This does not sound very convincing, it is true, but in the old days many tales just as unlikely were told of famous men. At any rate the ballad begins with the lilting line:—

"King Arthur lives in merrie Carleile,"

and all that concerns us at the moment is that perhaps he really did live there, and did do some very real fighting along the debateable line of the wall.

We next learn of Carlisle that King Egfrid of Northumbria rebuilt the city about the year 675, wherefore we can only suppose that it had suffered its somewhat usual fate, perhaps at the hands of that savage Saxon warrior called The Burner. But in any case, Carlisle never belonged to the Northumbrians for any considerable space of time, but was the capital of the Celtic or Welsh kingdom of Cumbria, from which the present name of Cumberland is derived.

In 875 the Danes had a turn at pillaging and harrying Carlisle, which was again in sorry plight. Both Cumbria and Northumbria were faring very badly in the struggle between the various kingdoms which then divided up Britain, and for a while it looked as if the energetic kings of the Scots would annex both these northern dominions. But the coming of the strong-handed Normans altered all this; and by far the most noteworthy event in the history of Carlisle was the fact that during 1092 and 1093 William Rufus seized Cumberland, and for the first time added it definitely to England.

Recognising at once the strength and value of Carlisle, Rufus caused a strong Norman castle to be built where the old Roman fort used to stand. To-day, despite the many rough adventures which have befallen this northern city, there yet remain portions of William Rufus's castle, side by side with fragments of the old Roman walls. Many of the modern buildings put up in King George's day are crumbling, but the old Norman and Roman remains are firm as a rock!

The castle was strengthened by King Henry I., but this did not prevent its seizure in 1135 by King David of Scotland, who added to it in turn. The Scots held the keep till 1157, when it was retaken by Henry II., but a few years later, in 1173, William the Lion, King of Scotland, besieged it, and for the next fifty years it changed hands several times, according to the fortunes of war. It is significant that a main street in the northern part of Carlisle is called "Scotch Street," while another in the southern part is called "English Street!"

Edward I. held a parliament here after defeating Wallace at Falkirk; and it was from Carlisle that this English King conducted his later operations against Scotland. It is a pathetic picture, that of this stern warrior in his old age, on his last march, trying to carry out his pet scheme of uniting the entire island under one rule. He was so ill that he had to be carried in a litter as far as Carlisle. Finding himself again so near the border, he felt the old fire glow within him, and sprang upon his horse—but at Burgh-on-Sands, on the shore of the Solway, whence he could view the goal of his ambition, the brave King died.

During the next thirty years Carlisle was frequently attacked by the Scots, but they were usually defeated.

In 1337, however, they partly, and in 1345 almost entirely burnt it down. Again in 1380 they burnt part of what had been rebuilt! Had there been fire insurance in these wild days, the premiums in Carlisle would have been heavy!

After the Wars of the Roses, the city seemed to settle down somewhat, and was chiefly known on the Border as the place where Scottish freebooters were hanged if caught. In one of the Border villages there is a famous churchyard where of old only the graves of women and children were to be seen. The explanation was given to a passing traveller by an old woman, who said that the men were all buried "in merrie Carlisle," meaning, that is, that they had all been hanged there!

In 1537 there was a rising in England known as the "Pilgrimage of Grace," in opposition to the savage policy of Henry's minister, Thomas Cromwell, and no less than eighty thousand insurgents are said to have attacked Carlisle; but after much fighting the rebels were defeated and seventy-four of their leaders were executed on the city walls.

When Mary Queen of Scots was imprisoned in Carlisle in 1568 it was vainly besieged by a force that sought to rescue her; but less than thirty years afterwards, in 1596, by a bold stroke of daring, Lord Scott of Buccleuch succeeded in surprising the castle and in liberating the well-known freebooter, "Kinmont Willie."

When King James united England and Scotland, the troubles of Carlisle might have been thought to be over. But in the civil war between King and Parliament it was again a storm centre, and was held alternately by each of the parties.

The last warlike operations against this much-besieged city were undertaken in 1745, when it was first taken by Prince Charlie, who made a triumphal entry without any serious fighting, and afterwards retaken almost as easily by the cruel Duke of Cumberland, whose entry into the place was followed, as usual, by a series of executions.

Among those who suffered was Sir A. Primrose, a gallant ancestor of the present Lord Rosebery. The victims were executed, with the cruelties of the old law against treason, on the celebrated Gallows Hill, at Harraby, and were buried in nameless graves in the Kirkyard of St Cuthbert's. Passing down the Botchergate (the London Road), past the site of the old Roman cemetery, the wayfarer may see Gallows Hill rise where a deep cut has been made to avoid a steep rise in the road. It was just outside the boundary of old Carlisle, and executions were witnessed from the walls, by men and women alike. Climb the hill—it is worth while. The little river Petteril sparkles at our feet; the view, fresh and green, stretches away nobly to the Pennines and the Border Hills. Keep a warm thought in your heart for all the gallant fellows who met death bravely in this place.

No history of Carlisle could omit to mention the Cathedral. English cathedrals are shaped like a cross lying on the ground; the long stem of the cross is the *nave* of the cathedral; the two arms are the *transepts*; and the upper end that continues the main stem is the *choir*. Where choir, nave and transepts meet, the *tower* rises. But unlike every other English cathedral, that of Carlisle has height and width, but is too short in length, two-thirds of the nave having been hurled down by the Scots!

Every cathedral has its history written in its stones, for those who know how to read it. That of Carlisle shows a stormy history, stormier than any other. It is not a peaceful building carried out very much in one style and undisturbed. It is a building full of signs of disturbance, the builders of which were interrupted in their plans by war and frequently had their building seriously damaged by their enemies. It is a mixture of styles, a mass of re-buildings and afterthoughts, but for that very reason it is a fitting symbol of the much-harassed city. With all its signs of storm and stress it has much beauty, and possesses the finest window in all England, one of the finest in the world. Just outside the Cathedral is a noble stretch of the old West Wall of the city, which gives a vivid idea of its strength in the old days.

The bishops of Carlisle live at Rose Castle, five miles south of the Cathedral. This has been their residence for over six hundred years. No doubt they thought it advisable not to live in the " merrie city " !

In this castle King Edward I. stayed. It was once partly burnt by Bruce, and again partly by the Puritans, but this is a comparatively clean record for such a district! In 1745 Captain Macdonald and his Scots came down to besiege it, but hearing that the bishop's baby daughter was about to be christened, the gallant captain would not let warfare spoil so peaceful a ceremony, and not only withdrew his men, but also left a white cockade behind him as a sign that the place was not to be molested. In all this he showed that true courtesy that always marks the real Highland gentleman.

Standing to-day in this bustling, breezy, pleasant little city, it is not easy to realise the wild scenes it has witnessed. The charming rivers that hem it in show no traces of the bloodshed of the past. Yet here have contended painted Pict and war-trained Roman ; here the most skilful leaders of the Celts, Saxons, and Danes have led their brave and sturdy men to battle; here Norman knight has fought with hardy Scot, and fierce Border factions have wrangled and sought speedy justice; Puritan has fought Cavalier, and Jacobite has faced Hanoverian; kings, generals, and warriors of many centuries have found a fitting meeting-place before or behind the walls of Carlisle.

An open, airy, quaint city. There is not very much that is old in it, for the old was not allowed to stand long enough! But on the top of its principal hill the tall truncated Cathedral presents a picturesque figure, and if we stand there or by the castle the eye commands fine, ancient walls and very delightful distances. It is a place of lingering memories, and if these are chiefly of strife and bloodshed we do not forget that to the Border folk the city was "Merrie Carlisle."

Chapter XXVII

Kinmont Willie

"O have ye not heard of the false Sakelde,
O have ye not heard of the keen Lord Scroope,
How they have taken bold Kinmont Willie
On Haribee to hang him oop?"

THE story of this famous freebooter, William Armstrong of Kinmonth, belongs to the time of Queen Elizabeth, when Lord Scroope was Warden of the Western Marches, and Mr Sakelde of Corby Castle was his Deputy.

Kinmont Willie was a descendant of the famous Johnie Armstrong of Gilnockie, and his capture was a violation of the existing truce between Scroope and Buccleuch, the Keeper of Liddesdale. Elizabeth was indignant at Buccleuch's action in rescuing Willie, and as the Scots at that time were very anxious not to offend her, Buccleuch was sent to England and came before the Queen, who asked him how he dared to undertake such an adventure. "What is it," answered he, "that a man dare not do?"

"With ten thousand such men," said Elizabeth, turning to a lord-in-waiting, "our brother of Scotland might shake the firmest throne of Europe."

The ballad tells of the capture of Kinmont Willie, and how the false Sakelde and his men treacherously seized him.

They bound his legs beneath his horse, and tied his hands behind his back, and with five men on each side to guard him, brought him over Liddel ford and through Carlisle sands to Carlisle castle.

When he arrived there, Willie addressed his captor in these words :

" My hands are tied, but my tongue is free. Who will avow this deed or answer for it to bold Buccleuch ? "

" Hold thy tongue, thou rank robber ! Never a Scot shall set thee free. Ye shall take farewell of me before ye cross my castle gate," said Scroope.

" Fear ye not that, my lord," answers Willie, " for by the faith of my body, never did I yet lodge in a hostelry but that I paid my reckoning before I went."

Word was sent to Branksome Hall to the Keeper of Liddesdale that Lord Scroope had captured Kinmont Willie, whereupon the Keeper smote the table with his hand till the red wine sprang on high, " A curse on my head," he cried, " if I be not avenged of Lord Scroope. Is my helmet a widow's cap, or my lance a twig from a willow-tree, or my fist a lady's lily hand, that an English lord should appraise me so lightly ? Have they taken Kinmont Willie in spite of the truce, and forgotten that the bold Buccleuch is Keeper on the Scottish side ? Have they taken Kinmont Willie so fearlessly, and forgotten that the bold Buccleuch can back a steed and wield a weapon ? Were there but war between the lands, then would I slight Carlisle Castle though it were built of marble ; I would set it on fire and drench it with English blood. But since there is peace and not war, I'll set the Kinmont free yet never harm English lad or lass ! "

So Buccleuch called forty bold Marchmen, all of his own name and kin except one, Sir Gilbert Elliot, Laird of Stobs. They came spur on heel and armour on shoulder, with gloves of green and feathers of blue. Five and five came first with hunting-horns and bugles; five and five more came with Buccleuch like Warden's men arrayed for battle; five and five came like a gang of masons, carrying long high ladders; and five and five came like broken men, and so they reached Woodhouselee.

When they had crossed to the English side, the first man they met was the false Sakelde.

"Where are ye going, ye keen hunters?" quoth Sakelde.

"We go to hunt an English stag that has trespassed on Scottish ground."

"Where are ye going, ye martial men?"

"We go to catch a rank robber that has broken faith with the bold Buccleuch."

"Where are ye going, ye mason lads, with all these long high ladders?"

"We go to harry a corbie's nest not far from here."

"Where are ye going, ye broken men?" said false Sakelde.

But Dickie of Dryhope, leader of the broken men, had never a word of learning, and answered nothing.

"Why trespass ye on the English side? Stand! ye raw-footed outlaws!"

Never a word yet said Dickie, but for answer ran his lance clean through the body of the false Sakelde.

On then they went to Carlisle town, crossing the Eden at Staneshaw-bank, nor lost they either horse or man, though the water was high in flood.

When they reached Staneshaw-bank the wind was rising, and the Laird ordered them to leave there their horses for fear they should stamp and neigh. The wind blew loudly enough then, but when they came beneath the castle wall there was wind and rain and flying sleet. On

The Escape of Kinmont Willie

they crept on their knees and held their breath till they placed the ladders against the wall. Buccleuch himself mounted first, took the watchman by the throat and flung him down upon the leads. " Thou hadst gone on the other side," said he, " had there not been peace between our lands."

" Sound out the trumpets ! " quoth he ; " let's wake up Lord Scroope ! " Then loud blew the Warden's trumpet to the tune of " O wha dare meddle wi' me ? "

To work they went speedily, and cut a hole through the lead, gaining thus the castle hall.

Those inside thought the castle had been taken by King James and all his men, yet it was only twenty Scots and ten that had put a thousand in such a stir. They hammered and banged at the bars until they came to the inner prison, where lay Kinmont Willie.

" Do ye sleep or wake, Kinmont Willie, on the morn when ye shall die ? "

"O I sleep lightly and wake often; it's long since sleep was frightened from me. Give my service to my wife and bairns and all good fellows that enquire after me."

Red Rowan, the strongest man in Teviotdale, lifted him up. " Stay now, Red Rowan, till I take farewell of Lord Scroope. Farewell, farewell, my good Lord Scroope," he cried. " I will pay ye for my lodging when first we meet on the Border."

With shout and cry Red Rowan bore him on his shoulders down the long ladder, the irons clanking at every stride.

" Many a time," said Kinmont Willie, " have I ridden a horse both wild and unruly, but never have my legs bestrode a rougher beast than Red Rowan. Many a time have I pricked a horse over the furrows, but never since I backed a steed have I worn such cumbrous spurs."

Scarcely had they won the Staneshaw-bank when all the bells in Carlisle were ringing and Lord Scroope was after them with a thousand men on horse and on foot. But—

"Buccleuch has turn'd to Eden water
Even where it flowed frae bank to brim,
And he has plunged in wi' a' his band,
And safely swam them through the stream.

He turn'd him on the other side,
And at Lord Scroope his glove flung he—
'If ye like na my visit to merry England,
In fair Scotland come visit me!'

All sore astonished stood Lord Scroope,
He stood as still as rock of stane;
He scarcely dared to trew[1] his eyes,
When through the water they had gane.

'He is either himsell a devil frae hell,
Or else his mother a witch maun be;
I wadna have ridden that wan water,
For a' the gowd[2] in Christentie.'"

[1] Trust. [2] Gold

Chapter XXVIII

Dick o' the Cow

"Fair Johnie Armstrong to Willie did say
'Billie, a-riding we will gae.'"

THE ballad of this name, a popular one in Liddesdale, relates, like that of Kinmont Willie, to the time when Lord Scroope was Warden of the West Marches and Governor of Carlisle. Dick o' the Cow seems to have been his fool or jester. Dickie, some years after the events described in the ballad, fell a victim to the vengeance of the Armstrongs.

There had been no raids from Liddesdale for a considerable time, and no riding, and the horses had all grown so fat that they dare scarcely stir out of the stall. Then fair Johnie Armstrong said to his brother Willie, "Brother, we will go a-riding. We have long been at feud with England, and perhaps we shall find some spoil."

So they rode to Hulton Hall and round about it, but the laird, a wise man, had left neither goods nor cattle outside to steal, except six sheep in a meadow. Said Johnie, "I'd rather die in England than take those six sheep to Liddesdale."

"But who was that man we last met as we came over the hill?"

"Oh, he is an innocent fool, and men call him Dick o' the Cow."

"That fool has three good cows of his own, as good as there are in Cumberland. Betide me life or death, they shall go to Liddesdale with me!"

So they came to the house of the poor fool, broke down his thick wall, loosed his three cows, and took also three coverlets from his wife's bed.

In the morning at daylight when the loss was discovered, there were loud lamentations. "Hold thy tongue, wife," said Dickie, "and stop thy crying. I'll bring thee back three cows for each one that thou hast lost."

So Dickie went to Lord Scroope. "Hold thy tongue, fool," said Scroope. "I have no time for jesting."

"A shame on your jesting, my lord!" said Dickie, "jesting agrees not with me. Liddesdale was in my house last night and has taken my three cows. I can no longer dwell in Cumberland as your poor faithful fool, unless you give me leave to steal in Liddesdale."

"I give thee leave, fool!" said Scroope; "but thou speakest against me and my honour unless thou give me thy hand and pledge that thou wilt steal from none but those who stole from thee."

"There is my right hand and pledge! May my head hang on Haribee, and may I never again cross Carlisle sands if I steal from any man who stole not from me."

Dickie joyfully took leave of his lord and master, and went and bought a bridle and a pair of new spurs which he packed up in the thigh of his breeches, then he came on as fast as he could to Pudding-burn house, where were thirty-three Armstrongs.

"O what has come to me now?" said Dickie, "what great trouble is this? For here is but one innocent fool against thirty-three Armstrongs?" Yet he went courteously up to the Hall board.

"Well may ye be, my good Laird's Jock, but the devil bless all your company. I'm come to complain of your man, Johnie Armstrong, and of his brother Willie, that they came to my house last night and took away my three cows."

Quoth fair Johnie Armstrong, "We'll hang him."

"Nay," said Willie, "we'll slay him."

But up spoke another young Armstrong, "We'll give him a thrashing and let him go."

Then up spoke the good Laird's Jock, the best fellow in all the company, "Sit down a while, Dickie, and we'll give thee a bit of thine own cow's thigh."

Dickie's heart was so sore that he could not eat a bit, but he went and lay down in an old peat-house where he thought to sleep the night, and all the prayers the poor fool prayed were, "I wish I had amends for my three good cows."

Now it was the custom of Pudding-burn house and of the house of Mangerton, whose laird was chief of the Armstrong clan, that any who came not to the table at the first summons got no more meat till the next meal, so some of the lads, hungry and weary, had thrown the key of the stable above the door-head. Dickie took good notice of that to turn it to his own account, went into the stable where stood thirty-three horses and tied thirty of them with St Mary's knot, tight to their stalls.

Of the remaining three, Dickie took two, which belonged to Johnie and Willie Armstrong, and the one belonging to the Laird's Jock he left loose in the stable. Leaping on one, he took the other along with him, and rode off as fast as he could.

When day came, there were great shouts and cries.

"Who has done this," quoth the good Laird's Jock; "see that ye tell me the truth."

"It is Dickie that has been in the stable last night, and has taken the horses."

"Ye never would listen to me," said the good Laird's Jock, "though I told ye true tales. Ye would never stay out of England but would steal everything, till ye were crooked and blind."

"Lend me thy bay," said fair Johnie; "he is the only horse loose in the stable, and I'll either fetch back Dick o' the Cow, or he shall die."

"Lend thee my bay!" said Jock; "he is worth gold and good money. Dick o' the Cow has taken two horses; I would not ye make them three."

Johnie, however, took the Laird's steel jacket on his back, and a two-handed sword by his side, and a steel cap on his head, and galloped after Dickie, who was barely three miles from the town when Johnie overtook him on Cannobie Lee, on the borders of Liddesdale.

"Abide, abide, thou traitor thief!" cried Armstrong; "the day is come that thou shalt die!"

Dickie looked over his left shoulder and said, "Johnie, hast thou no more in thy company? There is a preacher in our chapel who teaches all the livelong day, and when day is gone and night has come, there are only three words I remember—the first and second are Faith and Conscience—the third is 'Ne'er let a traitor free.' What faith and conscience was thine, Johnie, when thou tookest away my three cows? And when thou hadst taken them away, thou wast not satisfied. Thou sentest thy brother Willie, and took away three coverlets off my wife's bed!"

Then Johnie let his spear fall low by his side, and thought he would have killed Dickie, but the powers above were stronger than he, and he only succeeded in running through the fool's jerkin. Dickie out with his sword and ran after him, and when he could not get at him with the blade, he felled him with the butt-end over the eye, felled Johnie Armstrong, the finest man in the south country. "Gramercy," said Dickie, "I had but two horses, thou hast made them three!"—and he took Johnie's steel jacket off his back and his two-handed sword, and his steel cap. "Farewell, Johnie," said he, "I'll tell my master I met thee."

When Johnie wakened out of his swoon, he was a sad man. "Art thou gone, Dickie?" he said. "Then the shame and woe are left with me. Art thou gone? Then, Dickie, the devil go in thy company, for if I live to be a hundred, I'll never again fight with a fool."

Dickie came home to the good Lord Scroope as fast as he could. "Now, Dickie, I'll neither eat nor drink till thou art hanged on high." "Shame speed the liars, my lord," said Dickie, "this was not the promise ye made me, for I would never have gone to Liddesdale to steal if I had not got leave from thee." "But why did ye steal the Laird's Jock's horse? Ye might have lived long in Cumberland before the Laird's Jock had stolen from thee."

"Indeed, I knew ye lied, my lord. I won the horse from fair Johnie Armstrong hand to hand on Cannobie Lee. There is the jacket that was on his back, and the two-handed sword that hung by his side, and the steel cap that was on his head. I brought all these tokens to show thee."

"If that be true that thou tellest me (and I think thou durst not lie) I'll give thee fifteen pounds for the horse, all told out in the lap of thy cloak; I'll give thee one of my best milk cows to maintain thy wife and three children, and they will be as good as any two of thine would be."

"Shame speed the liars, my lord!" said Dickie. "Do ye think aye to make a fool of me? I'll either have twenty pounds for the horse or else I'll take him to Mortan fair."

So Scroope gave him twenty pounds for the horse, all in gold and good money, and one of his best milk cows to maintain his wife and three children.

Then Dickie rode as fast as he could through Carlisle town, and the first man he met was my lord's brother, Ralph Scroope, Bailiff of Glozenburrie.

"Well be ye met, Ralph Scroope!" said Dickie.

"Welcome, my brother's fool!" said Ralph. "Where did ye get Johnie Armstrong's horse?"

"Where did I get him? I stole him," said Dickie.

"Wilt thou sell me the bonny horse?"

"Ay, if thou count out the money in the lap of my cloak, for never a penny will I trust thee."

"I'll give thee ten pounds for the horse and count it into the lap of thy cloak, and one of my best milk cows to maintain thy wife and three children."

"Shame speed the liars, my lord! Do ye think aye to make a fool of me? I'll either have twenty pounds for the horse, or I'll take him to Mortan fair."

So Ralph gave him twenty pounds for the horse, all in gold and good money, and one of his milk cows to maintain his wife and three children.

Then Dickie leaped and laughed, and cried, "May the neck of the third horse be broken if either of the two were better than he!"

So he came home to his wife and ye may judge how the poor fool had succeeded. For her three stolen coverlets he gave her two score English pounds, and two cows as good as her own three. "And here," said he, "is a white-footed nag that I reckon will carry us both. But if I stay longer in Cumberland the Armstrongs will hang me." So Dickie took leave of his lord and went to live at Burgh under Stanmuir.

Chapter XXIX

The Lochmaben Harper

THE castle of Lochmaben is said to have been the residence of Robert Bruce while Lord of Allandale. Hence, as a royal fortress, the keeping of it was always granted to some powerful lord. There is extant a grant giving to one of these, Robert Lauder, the office of Captain and Keeper of Lochmaben Castle for seven years, and among his perquisites were " lands stolen from the King " !

The inhabitants of four small villages near the castle have each still to this day a right to a small piece of ground. These people are descendants of Robert Bruce's retainers, to whom he assigned these portions of land in reward for faithful service, and there are still to be found some families (*e.g.* the Richardsons of Lochmaben) who hold their lands direct from the times of Bruce without a break.

"O heard ye na o' the silly blind Harper,
How long he lived in Lochmaben town?
And how he wad gang to fair England,
To steal the Lord Warden's Wanton Brown?

But first he gaed to his gude wyfe,
Wi' a' the haste that he could thole[1]
'This wark,' quo' he, 'will ne'er gae well
Without a mare that has a foal.'

[1] Suffer.

Quoth his wife, "Thou hast a good grey mare that can jump both high and low; so set thee on her back and leave the foal at home with me." Away went the Harper to England as fast as he might, and when he came to Carlisle gate, who should be there but the Warden himself?

"'Come into my hall, thou silly blind Harper,
And of thy harping let me hear!'
'O, by my sooth,' quo' the silly blind Harper,
'I wad rather hae stabling for my mare.'

The Warden looked o'er his left shoulder,
And said unto his stable groom—
'Gae take the silly blind Harper's mare,
And tie her beside my Wanton Brown.'"

So the Harper harped and sang, the lordlings danced, and so sweet was the music that the groom forgot all about the stable door. Still the Harper harped on till all the nobles were fast asleep, when he quickly took off his shoes, crept softly down the stair, and hied with light tread to the stable door, which he opened and entered. He found there three-and-thirty steeds. He took a colt's halter which he had hidden in his hose, slipped it over Wanton Brown, tied it to the grey mare's tail, and turned them both loose at the castle gate.

Away they went over moor and moss and dale, and the mare never let Wanton rest a moment, but kept him galloping home to her foal. So swift of foot was she, and knew her way so well, that she reached Lochmaben a good three hours before daybreak.

When she came to the Harper's door, she neighed and snorted. "Rise up," shouted the Harper's wife, "thou lazy lass, and let in thy master and his mare." The lass rose up, put on her clothes and looked through the lock-hole. "By my sooth," cried she, "our mare has got a fine brown foal!"

"Hold thy tongue, thou foolish wench, the light is dazzling thine eyes. I'll wager all I have against a groat that it's bigger than ever our foal will be."

Still in merry Carlisle the Harper harped to high and low, and nought could they do but listen to him until day-dawn. But when it was daylight they discovered that Wanton Brown was gone and also the poor blind Harper's mare.

"Alas! alas!" cried the cunning old Harper, "alas that I came here; in Scotland I have lost a brown colt foal and in England they have stolen my good grey mare."

"Cease thy lamenting, thou silly blind Harper, and go on harping; we'll pay thee well for the loss of thy colt foal and thou shalt have a far better mare." So the harper harped and sang, and so sweet were his harpings that he was paid for the foal he never had lost and three times over for the gray mare.

Chapter XXX

The Rookhope Ride

THIS Durham border song is supposed to be spoken by a Weardale man, who begins by denouncing the inhabitants of the Tyne valley, "and all their companies there about" as false thieves,

> "minded to do mischief
> And at their stealing stands not out."

It must be confessed that the Tynedale men had an unenviable reputation. They were such lawless desperadoes, so addicted to rapine, that during more than two centuries the merchants of Newcastle regularly refused to take an apprentice born in that district. The date is December 1572. The rebel Earl of Northumberland, who had taken up arms for Mary Queen of Scots, and for the old religion, had been betrayed by the Scots and beheaded at York. Owing to this rebellion there was great confusion in the northern counties, hence the time was well chosen by the "limmer thieves" of Tynedale to make a predatory raid on their neighbours. They gathered together the stoutest men of arms and the best in gear, a hundred or more in number, and in the forenoon, about eleven o'clock, they came into a "byefell" and stopped for a meal—the last which some of them would eat. When they had eaten, they chose their captains, Harry Corbyl, Simon Fell, and Martin Ridley.

Then they rode on over the moss, " with many a brank and whew," saying to one another that they were men enough,

> " For Weardale-men have a journey ta'en,
> They are so far out o'er yon fell,
> That some of them's with the two earls,
> And others fast in Bernard castell.
>
> There we shall get gear enough,
> For there is nane but women at hame;
> The sorrowful fend that they can make.
> Is loudly cries as they were slain."

They came in at Rookhope Head, which is the top of a rocky valley, about five miles long, at the end of which Rookhope Burn empties itself into the river Wear. This valley is as wild and open to-day as it was then. In some four hours they gathered together about six hundred sheep and they were engaged in " shifting " the horses, when the hue and cry was raised by one Rowley, whose horse they tried to take. He was the first man to see them. The cry spread rapidly down Rookhope burn and through Weardale, and word came to the bailiff's house at the East-gate. He was out, but his wife had his horse saddled and sent it to him, together with his sword, spear, and jacket quilted with iron plates, the sort of harness worn by the moss-troopers and other light horsemen of the time. The bailiff had already heard the bad news, and was sorely troubled thereby. His own brother had been attacked three days before by marauders, and lay sick with nineteen wounds. Yet the bailiff shrank not at all, but hied fast after the sheep-stealers, with as many of the neighbours as he could gather to bear him company.

The pursuers overtook the thieves in Nuketon Cleugh,

and gave them all the fighting they wanted. Not one of them ever thought to see his wife again. They bore three banners against the Weardale men, "as if the world had been all their own." The fray lasted only an hour, but many a tall man lay weaponless and sore wounded before that hour was done, and four of the Northumbrian prickers were slain, including Harry Corbyl whom they had chosen to be their captain. Eleven of them were taken prisoners. Only one of the Weardale men fell but—

"These Weardale-men, they have good hearts,
They are as stiff as any tree;
For, if they'd everyone been slain,
Never a foot back man would flee.

And such a storm amongst them fell,
As I think you never heard the like;
For he that bears his head on high,
He oft-tymes falls into the dyke.

And now I do entreat you all,
As many as are present here,
To pray for the singer of this song,
For he sings to make blythe your cheer."

Chapter XXXI

Barthram's Dirge

THE story of how this ballad came to be preserved to us is a very interesting one. A Mr Surtees, who was very interested in the old ballads, used to give work to a poor old Scotswoman to weed in his garden. Finding that she had learnt ballads in her young days, he encouraged her to talk about them, and this was amongst those which she recited to him. She told him that it referred to a young man named Bertram or Barthrum, who made love to a young lady against the wish of her brothers. The cruel brothers slew him, but the lady had him buried at the very spot where he was wont to come to visit her in the days of their love. Sir Walter Scott thinks that perhaps Barthram was an Englishman and the lady was Scottish, and that the anger of the lady's brothers against him was partly on that account.

It must be remembered that in those stormy days, when Border rivalry was keen, and all the Border chiefs, on both sides, were men of war-like mould, intermarriage between the two races was punishable by Border law. Each side felt equally that such mixed marriages would sooner or later produce a race that was neither loyal English nor loyal Scotch. A spirit of aloofness and rivalry was deliberately encouraged, right up to the time of the union of the two countries under one king.

BARTHRAM'S DIRGE

They shot him dead at the Nine-Stone Rig,
  Beside the Headless Cross,
And they left him lying in his blood,
  Upon the moor and moss.

. . . .

They made a bier of the broken bough,
  The sauch and the aspin gray,
And they bore him to the Lady Chapel,
  And waked him there all day.

A lady came to that lonely bower,
  And threw her robes aside,
She tore her long yellow hair,
  And knelt at Barthram's side.

She bathed him in the Lady-Well,
  His wounds so deep and sair,
And she plaited a garland for his breast,
  And a garland for his hair.

They rowed him in a lily-sheet,
  And bare him to his earth,
And the Gray Friars sung the dead man's mass,
  As they pass'd the Chapel Garth.

They buried him at the mirk midnight,
 When the dew fell cold and still,
When the aspin gray forgot to play,
 And the mist clung to the hill.

They dug his grave but a bare foot deep,
 By the edge of the Ninestone Burn,
And they covered him o'er with the heather-flower,
 The moss and the Lady fern.

A Gray Friar staid upon the grave,
 And sang till the morning tide,
And a friar shall sing for Barthram's soul,
 While the Headless Cross shall bide.[1]

[1] Mr Surtees observes, on this passage, that in the return made by the commissioners, on the dissolution of Newminster Abbey, there is an item of a Chauntery, for one priest to sing daily *ad crucem lapideam*. Probably many of these crosses had the like expiatory solemnities for persons slain there. They certainly did bury, in former days, near the Ninestone Burn, for Sir Walter Scott found there, lying among the heather, a small monumental cross, with initials, which he reverently placed upright.

Chapter XXXII

Queen Mary and the Borders

THE brief reign of Mary, Queen of Scots, was so crowded with incident that she was left with little time to visit the disturbed borderland of her kingdom. None-the-less her few visits to this district were fraught with important consequences. In 1565, when she married her cousin Lord Darnley, the head of the Douglas faction and a Roman Catholic, the Protestant nobles took up arms. In her very honeymoon she headed her soldiers, pursued the rebels to Dumfries, entered the town with a pistol in each hand, and laughed heartily at the fun of making her enemies " skip like rabbits " over the Border. She was only twenty-two years old —a fearless, dashing, attractive woman, with a clever head, a strong will, and a wild and lawless disposition.

In the next year she again visited the Border, but on a very different errand. Mary had developed an extreme fancy for that bold Border Lord, the Earl of Bothwell, whose Castle of Hermitage commanded the picturesque and important valley of the Liddel. The Queen had given him authority to control the fierce Borderers; and when the earl was riding out he met the most lawless of them, Jock Elliot, of whom the couplet—

" My name is little Jock Elliot
And who dare meddle wi' me?"

Bothwell fired straight at Elliot with his pistol, wounding

Queen Mary crossing the Solway

him in the leg. Elliot aimed a mighty blow at Bothwell with his two-handed sword, giving the earl so sore a wound that he was glad enough to gallop home while there was yet time to save his life.

Mary was holding solemn court at Jedburgh when she heard of her favourite's danger. She straightway took horse and rode to Hermitage, a hard cross-country ride of twenty miles, through a district infested with reckless men. When she galloped back to Jedburgh, she was in high fever and nearly died. Later on, in the misery of her long imprisonment, she often said, "Would I had died at Jedburgh!" Years later, a broken piece of a silver spur was found at Queensmire, on this difficult and dangerous road, just where Queen Mary's horse was said to have come to grief.

Yet another time Queen Mary came to the Border, this time to cross it—after her imprisonment at Lochleven, her escape, and the disastrous rout of her followers at Langside. Daring and resourceful as ever, she fled across the Solway in an open boat; Scotland had failed her, she sought the protection of England. She landed at Cockermouth, and was led to Carlisle by Sir R. Lowther, and kept there, in reality a prisoner, while Elizabeth was musing of the dangers of the position. The Earls of Northumberland and Westmoreland took up Mary's cause and attempted to rescue her, but the Warden of Carlisle, Lord Scroope, defended the town successfully against the two earls, and they were soon in flight, eastward for their very lives. After this attempt at rescue Mary was, for greater safety, sent down to Bolton Castle in Yorkshire.

Leonard Dacre, a member of the powerful Cumberland family of the Dacres, seems to have played a treacherous part, first promising the earls his help, and then betraying them to Elizabeth. He seized Nawarth Castle, which properly belonged to his young niece, and collected together three thousand men to the old Border war-cry, "A Red Bull, a Red Bull!" (probably the nickname of some fierce red-haired Celtic champion). The defeated earls came to Nawarth for shelter, and Dacre refused to harbour them. But by this time Elizabeth was convinced of Dacre's treason, and ordered Lord Hudson, the Governor of Berwick, to arrest him.

Hudson appears to have marched by rather a roundabout way, for Dacre met him at Geltbridge, on the west of Nawarth. A bridge is always a good point of vantage for meeting an enemy, especially when the river runs, as the Gelt does, through a deep and wooded gorge. The enemy has only a narrow way by which to approach, and no doubt Dacre posted his archers behind the trees and among the great rocks. The fight was a desperate one, but Hudson's men prevailed and pursued their foes far up the hill of Gelt, scuffling fiercely among the forest trees and dyeing a deeper hue the red sandstone cliffs and quarries.

All the rebels who could escape fled across the Border to Scotland, where the Borderers, who were till then their enemies, received them with that open and fair hospitality which was one of their many great qualities. Elizabeth demanded that the leading noblemen should be given up to her; but although the Scottish Regent, Murray, made a pretence of trying to secure the Earl of Westmoreland, the Scots had too much sense of honour to allow him to proceed.

The Earl of Northumberland, was however betrayed to the Scottish Regent by Hector Armstrong of Harelaw; but this the gallant Borderers held to be shameful, and Armstrong was a ruined man from that day forth.

Two years later, this Earl was actually sold to Elizabeth and beheaded at York. Thus ended this small rebellion, called in history the Rising of the North, but which is known locally in Cumberland as Dacre's Raid.

There is a little stream which rushes down a deep and beautiful glade to join the river Gelt above Geltbridge; this stream is known as "Hellbeck," and villagers tell us that the reason for this name is that it was stained with blood for two whole days after some battle that took place there. This battle is probably the one spoken of here.

A wicket gate by Geltbridge leads us to the path through Gelt woods. The noble gorge is deeply cleft through the grand red sandstone rocks. Below roars and dashes the impetuous river; the path winds, sometimes high, sometimes low, through wonderful weeds, carpeted with beautiful mosses, gemmed with delightful flowers. On one of the rocks is an inscription carved by a Roman soldier, over fifteen hundred years ago. Follow the river, up, up, till the little Hellbeck is seen trickling down from the east; cross the little bridge and follow the streamlet on its opposite bank, along a path so little trod as to be scarcely visible; wander among ferns along one of the loneliest glens in the whole of Britain, passing the great railway bridge (*under* if the stream be low or *over* if it be high) till you join the main road again. There is no spot more beautiful or more peaceful. Yet this is the Hellbeck where men fought and hacked, and slashed and slew, among these woods, up and down these steep hillsides. These old trees, when young, have felt warm blood at their roots; and all because of a young, wild wilful queen, who fascinated men's hearts then, and the memory of whom fascinates them still.

Chapter XXXIII

The Raid of the Reidswire

"To deal with proud men is but pain,
For either must ye fight or flee,
Or else no answer make again,
But play the beast, and let them be."

REIDSWIRE, the name of a place about ten miles from Jedburgh, means the Red Swire. Swire is an old northern term for the descent of a hill, and the epithet red may refer to the colour of the heath.

The affair about which we are to tell took place on the 7th of July 1575, at a meeting held, on a day of truce, by the Wardens of the Marches, for redressing wrongs and adjusting difficulties which could not be prevented from arising upon the Border. The Scottish Warden was Sir John Carmichael, and among his following were the Armstrongs and Elliots, Douglas of Cavers (a descendant of the Douglas who fell at Otterbourne), Cranstoun, whose ferocious motto was "Ye shall want ere I want," Gladstain, "good at need," and the ancient head of the Rutherfoords, called in tradition the Cock of Hunthill, "with his nine sons him about." The English Warden was the haughty Sir John Forster, and he had full fifteen hundred men with him, chiefly Northumbrians, Tynedale, and Reedsdale men, who looked with scorn upon the much smaller array of their hereditary foes.

The meeting, however, began meekly enough, with merriment and jests. Such Border meetings of truce, though they might wind up in blood, as was to happen now, always began as occasions of marketing and revelry. Both parties came fully armed to such a tryst, yet intermixed in mutual sports and familiar intercourse,

"Some gaed to drink, and some stood still,
And some to cards and dice them sped."

The Scots planted their pavilions or tents and feared no ill, even when they saw five hundred Fenwicks (a powerful Northumbrian clan) "marching in a flock." The clerk began to call the rolls, and to deal with one complaint after another for the loss of cows or ewes or other property. In the course of the proceedings an accusation was raised against an English freebooter named Farnstein, at the instance of a Scotch complainant. A "true bill" was found against the man, which means that he ought to be handed over to justice. But the English Warden alleged that he had fled, and could not be found. Carmichael, considering this as a pretext to avoid making compensation for the felony, bade the Northumbrians speak out plainly, and "cloke no cause for ill nor good." Upon this Sir John Forster, a proud and insolent man, "began to reckon kin and blood," by which picturesque phrase the ballad probably means that he swiftly added up his forces. Then he drew himself up, backed by his Dalesmen, all fingering their bows, and with insulting expressions against Carmichael's kin he bade him "match with his equals." The men of Tynedale, who only wanted a pretext for a quarrel, drew their bows and let off a flight of arrows among the Scots. The more moderate men on both sides at first tried to quell the tumult, but in vain. The fight was bound to come.

> "Then there was naught but bow and spear,
> And every man pulled out a brand."

The English showed their usual dexterity with the bow. The Scots, for some reason, never took to this weapon; they had fire-arms, pistolets, and the like. The terrible cloth-yard arrows "from tackles flew," and the old proverb bade fair to justify itself, that every English archer carried twenty-four Scots under his belt—an allusion to his bundle of shafts. Success seemed certain for the English side; some of the foremost men among the Scots fell, and even Carmichael was thrown to the ground and was within an ace of being made a prisoner. The air resounded with the rallying cries of the English, the names of their captains, "A Shaftoe! A Shaftoe!" "A Fenwick! A Fenwick!" The Scots had little harness among them, only a few had the jack which served them as a defence for the body. Nevertheless, they laid about them sturdily, with "dints full dour," and there was many a cracked crown. Then suddenly a shout was heard. "Jedburgh's here!" A body of Jedburgh burgesses appear to have arrived just in the nick of time to add to the outnumbered force of Scots. They probably wore armour and what were called "white hats," that is steel caps. Meanwhile, the English, too confident of easy victory, instead of slaying more Scots and turning the repulse into a rout, thought only to plunder the unhappy merchants, who, trusting to the truce which had been proclaimed, had attached themselves to the meeting. Had it not been for the English greed, the Scots would have been defeated. As it was, the Tynedale men, throwing themselves on the merchants' packs, fell into disorder, their adversaries recovered from their surprise, and the timely arrival of the Jedburgh men turned the tables. A short, sharp bout ended in the triumph of the Scots and the Northumbrians fled, "Down ower the brae, like clogged bees." The Scots took many prisoners, amongst whom were the English Warden, and his son-in-law, Sir Francis Russell; but the most gallant soldier taken that day was that courteous knight, Sir Cuthbert Collingwood, to whose family Admiral Collingwood belonged. Several of those "Fenwicks fierce," who had turned up five hundred strong at the commencement of the fray, had the mortification of being carried off in triumph by their enemies. All these prisoners were sent to the Earl of Morton, Regent of Scotland, who detained them at Dalkeith for some days, until the bitter feeling natural after such an affair had died down, at any rate in part, and by this prudent precaution the Regent is thought to have probably averted a war between the two kingdoms. He ultimately permitted them to return to their own country, parting from them with great expressions of regard. The interest taken in the matter by Queen Elizabeth, and the representations of her Ambassador at Edinburgh, no doubt had something to do with this happy issue.

It will probably occur to the careful reader of this book as somewhat strange to find the ruling powers of England and Scotland both so set upon peace; but it must be remembered that at this period in the reign of Queen Elizabeth the heir-apparent to the English throne was the young James VI., King of Scotland, who would naturally not wish for any quarrel with the country which he hoped later on to rule. Elizabeth, on the other hand, had Mary Queen of Scots as her prisoner, and did not wish in any further way to strain the already delicate relations between the two countries.

The Carmichael mentioned in this ballad, known in full as Sir John Carmichael of Edrom, Scottish Warden of the Middle Marches, was afterwards murdered by one of the wild Armstrongs, who is said to have composed, the night before his execution, the following manly and pathetic "Good-night." The third and fourth lines show clearly the disrepute into which this once honoured clan was falling; the seventh and eighth lines could only have been written by one who, despite his faults, had the true gallant instincts deep in his blood.

ARMSTRONG'S GOOD-NIGHT

"This night is my departing night,
For here nae langer must I stay;
There's neither friend nor foe o' mine,
But wishes me away.

What I have done thro' lack of wit,
I never, never can recall;
I hope ye're a' my friends as yet;
Good-night and joy be with you all!"

Chapter XXXIV

Jock o' the Side

"He is well kend, John of the Syde,
A greater thief did never ryde."

THE subject of this ballad bears some resemblance to Kinmont Willie, and such adventures were not uncommon in those turbulent times. The events we are to relate originated in a raid ridden by the famous Liddesdale spearmen (the hardiest of the Scotch moss-troopers) upon English ground.

"They had better hae staid at home," for the outcome was that one of their best men, Michael of Winfield, was killed, and Jock o' the Side, nephew to the Laird of Mangerton, was taken prisoner, and promptly lodged in Newcastle Jail. When the news reached Jock's mother she kilted her coats up to her knee, and ran down the water with the tears falling in torrents from her eyes. She ran to Mangerton House, on the banks of the Liddel, and told her brother, the good old lord, the bad news. "Michael is killed, and they have taken my son John." "Never fear, sister," quoth Mangerton, "I have eighty-three yokes of oxen, my barns, my byres, my folds are all filled, I'll part with them all ere Johnie shall die." Then he thought out his plan. "Three men I'll send to set him free, all harnessed in the best steel; the English loons shall feel the weight of their broad swords. The Laird's

Jock shall be one, the Laird's Wat two, and Hobbie Noble, thou must be the third. Thy coat is blue, and since England banished thee thou hast been true to me." Now this Hobbie was an Englishman, born in Bewcastle-dale, the wildest district in Cumberland. Like numerous other English outlaws, he had made his own country too hot to hold him; his misdeeds had banished him to Liddesdale, and he was now in high favour with the Laird of Mangerton. The Laird gave the dauntless three orders to reverse the shoes of their horses, so that anyone crossing their trail might think they were proceeding in a contrary direction. He also warned them not to seem gentlemen, but to look like corn-carriers; not to show their good armour, nor appear like men of war, but to be arrayed as country lads, with halter and cart-collar on each mare. So Hobbie mounted his grey, Jack his lively bay, and Wat his white horse, and they rode for Tyne water. When they reached the Tyne they lighted down at a ford, and by the moonlight they cut a tree, with fifteen nogs on each side, to serve them as a scaling ladder, to climb Newcastle wall with. However, when they came to Newcastle town and alighted at the wall, their tree proved three ells too short, and there was nothing for it but to force the gates. At the gate a proud porter attempted to withstand them. The Armstrongs wrung his neck, took his life and his keys at once, and cast his body behind the wall. Soon they reached the jail, and called to the prisoner,

"Sleeps thou, wakes thou, Jock o' the Side,
Or art thou weary of thy thrall?"

Jock answered dolefully, "Often I wake, nay, sleep seldom comes to me—but who's this knows my name so well?" Then out and spoke the Laird's

Jock, his cousin and namesake, "Now fear ye not, my billie!" quoth he; "for here are the Laird's Jock, the Laird's Wat, and Hobbie Noble the Englishman come to set you free." Jock o' the Side did not think it possible that they could effect his release. "Now hold thy tongue, my good cousin," said he. "This cannot be—

'For if all Liddesdale were here the night,
The morn's the day that I mnst die.'

They have laid full fifteen stone of Spanish iron on me, I am fast bound with locks and keys in this dark and dreary dungeon." But the Laird's Jock replied. "Fear not that; faint heart never won fair lady. Work thou within, we'll work without, and I'll be sworn we'll set thee free." They loosed the first strong door without a key, the next chained door they split to flinders. The Laird's Jock got the prisoner on his back, irons and all, and brought him down the stairs with no small speed and joy. Hobbie Noble offered to bear some of his weight, but the Laird's Jock said that he was lighter than a flea. When they had all gone out at the gates, the prisoner was set on horseback, and they all joked wantonly. "O Jock," they cried, "you ride like a winsome lady, with your feet all on one side." The night was wet, but they did not mind. They hied them on full merrily until they came to the ford at Cholerford, above Hexham. There the water was running mountains high. They asked an old man, "Honest man, tell us in haste, will the water ride?" "I've lived here thirty years and three," replied he, "and I never saw the Tyne so big, nor running so like a sea." The Laird's Wat counselled them to halt. "We need not try it, the day is come we all must die!" "Poor faint-hearted thief!" cried the Laird's Jock. "There'll no man die but him that's fated ; I'll guide you safely through ; lift the prisoner behind me." With that they took to the water and managed to swim through. "Here we are all safe," said the Laird's Jock triumphantly. "Poor faint Wat, what think ye now ?" They now saw twenty men pursuing them, sent from Newcastle, all English lads, stout and true. But when their leader saw the water he shook his head. "It won't ride, my lads," said he. Then he cried to the party of Scots : "Take the prisoner, but leave me my fetters." But the Laird's Jock was not a Scot for nothing. "I wat weel no," he shouted back, "I'll keep them, they'll make horse-shoes for my mare—for I am sure she's bought them right dear from thee." Then they went on their way to Liddesdale, as fast as they could, and did not rest until they had brought the rescued prisoner to his own fireside, and made him free of his irons.

Chapter XXXV

Hobbie Noble

"Keep ye weel frae the traitor Mains!
For gold and gear he'll sell ye a'."

IN the ballad of "Jock o' the Side," we have seen Hobbie Noble act a distinguished part in the deliverance from captivity of Jock, cousin of the Laird of Mangerton, chief of the Armstrong clan. Now in the following ballad we shall learn how ungrateful the Armstrongs were for his faithful services. The Armstrongs were one of those outlawed or broken clans, whose hand was against every man, and living as they did in what was called the Debateable Land, on the frontier between Liddesdale and England, these stark cattle-lifters and arrant thieves levied tribute from English and Scotch alike. Halbert or Hobbie Noble was an Englishman, a Cumbrian born and bred, but his misdeeds were so great, they banished him never to return, and he established himself among the Armstrongs. From their territory he continued his depredations upon the English, in resentment of which they at length offered a bribe to the Armstrongs to decoy him into England under pretence of inviting him to join them in a foray.

"At Kershope foot the tryst was set,
Kershope of the lily lee,"

and the name of the chief traitor and leader of the gang

was Sim o' the Mains. Hobbie harnessed himself "both with the iron and with the steel," buckled spur on his heel and belted brand to his side, leaped upon his "fringed grey," and rode down the banks of the Liddel. As soon as he saw the others, "Well be ye met, my comrades five," he cried. "Now, what is your will with me?" They all answered, with one consent, "Thou'rt welcome here, brave Noble; wilt thou ride with us into England, and we will be thy safe warrant? If we get a horse worth a hundred pounds thou shalt soon be upon its back." But Hobbie said that he dared not ride into England by day, as he had a feud with the Land-Sergeant (an officer under the Warden, to whom was entrusted the arrest of delinquents).

"But will ye stay till the day gae down,
Until the night come o'er the ground,
And I'll be a guide worth any two
That may in Liddesdale be found?
Though the night be black as pitch and tar,
I'll guide ye o'er yon hill so high;
And bring ye all in safety back,
If ye'll be true and follow me."

They let him guide them over moss and moor, over hill and hope, and over many a down, until they came to the Foulbogshiel. But meanwhile word was gone to the Land-Sergeant, in Askerton, about seventeen miles from Carlisle. "The deer that you have hunted so long, is in Bewcastle Waste this day." The Sergeant understood at once. Quoth he, "Hobbie Noble is that deer! He carries the style full high. He has often driven our bloodhounds back. Now go, warn the bows of Hartlie Burn, see they sharpen their arrows on the wall! Warn Willeva and Speir Edom, take word to them that they meet me on the Rodric-haugh at break of day. We will on to Conscouthart-green, for there, I think, we'll get our quarry." In the meantime Hobbie had alighted and was sleeping in the Foulbogshiel. He dreamed that his horse was shot beneath him, and he himself was hard put to it to get away. The cocks crowed, the day dawned, and if Hobbie had not wakened he would have been taken or slain in his sleep.

> "Awake, awake, my comrades five !
> I trow here makes a full ill day ;
> Yet the worst cloak o' this company
> I hope shall cross the Waste this day."

Thus cried he to his companions, thinking the gates were clear. But alas ! it was not so. They were beset by the Land-Sergeant's men, cruel and keen, and while the Englishmen came before, the traitor Sim o' the Mains came behind. Had Noble been as masterful a champion as Wallace himself, he could not have won under such untoward circumstances. He had but a laddie's sword, but he did more than a laddie's deeds, for that sword would have cleared Conscouthart-green had it not broken over one of the English heads. So his treacherous companions delivered Hobbie up to the officers of justice; they bound him with his own bowstring, but what made his heart feel sorest of all, was that it was his own five who bound him. They took him on to Carlisle. They asked him mockingly if he knew the way. He thought much, but said little, though he knew it as well as they did. As they took him up the Carlisle streets, the old wives cast their windows wide, every woman whispering to another, "That's the man loosed Jock o' the Side." The poor fellow cried out, "Fie on ye, women! why call ye me man ? It's no like a man that I'm used, but like a beaten hound that's been fighting in the gutter." They had him up through Carlisle town, and set him by a chimney fire, where they gave him a wheaten loaf to eat, and a can of beer. "Confess my lord's horse, Hobbie," they said, "and to-morrow in Carlisle thou shalt not die." "How can I confess them," says the poor man, "when I never saw them." And he swore a great oath, by the day that he was born, that he had never had anything of my lord's. He had but short shrift and they hung him the next morning.

According to the ballad, his last words were of manly pride:—

> "Yet wad I rather be ca'd Hobbie Noble,
> In Carlisle, where he suffers for his fault,
> Than I'd be ca'd the traitor Mains,
> That eats and drinks o' meal and malt."

Thus died the doughty Noble. It is proper to add, however, that the Armstrong's chief, Lord Mangerton, with whom Hobbie had been a favourite, took a severe revenge on the traitors who betrayed him. The contriver of the scheme, Sim o' the Mains, fled into England to escape the resentment of his chief, and was there caught by the English, and himself executed at Carlisle, two months after Hobbie's death in the same place! Such is, at least, the tradition of Liddesdale.

Chapter XXXVI

The Laird o' Logie

IN 1592, the Earl of Bothwell, Francis Stuart, failed in an attempt against King James VI., whom he tried to surprise in the palace of Falkland. Amongst his adherents, whom he sought about the King's person, was the hero of this ballad, the Laird of Logie, who was taken prisoner and laid in Edinburgh chapel in the keeping of Sir John Carmichael, the hero of the ballad called the "Raid of Reidswire." Carmichael was at this time captain of the King's Guard, and had the keeping of State criminals.

I will sing, if ye will hearken,
If ye will hearken unto me;
The King has ta'en a poor prisoner,
The wanton laird o' young Logie.

Young Logie's laid in Edinburgh chapel,
Carmichael's the keeper o' the key;
And may Margaret's lamenting sair,
A' for the love of young Logie.

"Lament, lament na, may Margaret,
And of your weeping let me be;
For ye maun to the King himsell,
To seek the life of young Logie."

May Margaret has kilted her green cleiding,[1]
And she has curl'd back her yellow hair—
"If I canna get young Logie's life,
Farewell to Scotland for evermair."

When she came before the King,
She kneelit lowly on her knee—
"O what's the matter, may Margaret?
And what needs a' this courtesie?"

"A boon, a boon, my noble liege,
A boon, a boon, I beg o' thee!
And the first boon that I come to crave,
Is to grant me the life of young Logie."

"O na, O na, may Margaret,
Forsooth, and so it mauna be;
For a' the gowd o' fair Scotland
Shall not save the life of young Logie."

But she has stown[2] the King's redding kaim,[3]
Likewise the Queen her wedding knife,
And sent the tokens to Carmichael,
To cause young Logie get his life.

She sent him a purse of the red gowd,
Another o' the white monie;
She sent him a pistol for each hand,
And bade him shoot when he gat free.

When he came to the Tolbooth stair,
There he let his volley flee;

[1] Clothing. [2] Stolen. [3] Dressing comb.

"A boon, a boon, my noble liege,
A boon, a boon, I beg o' thee!"

It made the King in his chamber start,
E'en in the bed where he might be.

"Gae out, gae out, my merrymen a',
And bid Carmichael come speak to me;
For I'll lay my life the pledge o' that,
That yon's the shot o' young Logie."

When Carmichael came before the King,
He fell low down upon his knee;
The very first word that the King spake,
Was—"Where's the laird of young Logie?"

Carmichael turn'd him round about
(I wot the tear blinded his ee),
"There came a token frae your grace,
Has ta'en away the laird frae me."

"Hast thou play'd me that, Carmichael?
And hast thou play'd me that?" quoth he;
"The morn the justice-court's to stand,
And Logie's place ye maun supplie."

Carmichael's awa to Margaret's bower,
Even as fast as he may dree—
"O if young Logie be within,
Tell him to come and speak with me!"

May Margaret turn'd her round about
(I wot a loud laugh laughed she),
"The egg is chipp'd, the bird is flown,
'Ye'll see nae mair of young Logie."

Chapter XXXVII

Jamie Telfer of the Fair Dodhead

"'Tis I, Jamie Telfer, of the fair Dodhead,
And a harried man I think I be!
There's nothing left at the fair Dodhead
But a woeful wife and bairnies three!"

ABOUT Martinmas time, when Border steeds get corn and hay, the Captain of Bewcastle rode over to Tividale to forage. And first he met a guide high up in Hardhaughswire, and next he met a guide low down in Borthwick water.

"What tidings, what tidings, my trusty guide?"

"No tidings have I—yet if ye go to the fair Dodhead, I'll let ye see many a cow's calf." Right hastily they came to the fair Dodhead, loosed the cows and ransacked the house.

Jamie Telfer's [1] heart was sore when he saw this, and the tears ran down his cheeks, and he pleaded with the Captain to give him back his gear, or else he would have revenge upon him. But the Captain only laughed and said, "Man, there's nothing in thy house but an old sword without a sheath that could scarcely kill a mouse."

The sun was not up though the moon had gone down, and there was a sprinkling of new-fallen snow upon the

[1] The Telfers, though they had become Scotch at the time of this ballad, were originally a Norman family, descended from the knight "Taille-fer" (cut-iron), who came over with William the Conqueror.

ground when Jamie Telfer ran ten miles a-foot between the Dodhead and Stob's Hall. When he came to the tower gate he shouted aloud, and old Gibby Elliot came out and asked the meaning of such disturbance.

"It is I, Jamie Telfer, of the fair Dodhead, and a harried man am I, for nothing is left at fair Dodhead but a sad wife and three bairnies."

"Go and seek help at Branksome Hall, for ye shall get none from me—seek help where ye paid blackmail, for, man, never did ye pay *me* any."

James turned him about, his eyes blinded with tears. "Never shall I pay blackmail again to Elliot. My hounds may all run masterless, my hawks may fly as they will from tree to tree, and my lord may seize the lands of his vassal, for never shall I see again the fair Dodhead."

He turned him to Tiviotside and made as fast as he could for Coultart cleugh, and there he shouted aloud until out came old Jock Grieve, and asked who it was that made such a noise.

"It is I, Jamie Telfer, of the fair Dodhead, and a harried man am I, for nothing is left at fair Dodhead but a weeping wife and three bairnies, and six poor calves stand in the stall crying aloud for their mothers."

"Alack!" quoth Jock Grieve, "alack, my heart is sore for thee! for I married the eldest of three sisters, and you married the youngest."

So he took out his bonny black horse, right well fed with corn and hay, and set Jamie Telfer on his back, to take his troubles to Catslockhill. When he came to Catslockhill he shouted aloud until out came William's Wat to ask what was the matter.

"It is I, Jamie Telfer, of the fair Dodhead, and a harried man am I. The Captain of Bewcastle has driven away my gear; for God's sake rise and help me."

"Alas and alack," quoth William's Wat, "my heart is sore for thee. Never did I yet come to the fair Dodhead and found thy basket bare."

He set his two sons on coal-black steeds, and he himself mounted a freckled grey, and with Jamie they rode to Branksome Hall, where they shouted so loud and high that old Buccleuch came out to ask what was the matter.

"It is I, Jamie Telfer, of the fair Dodhead, and a harried man am I; there is nought left at fair Dodhead but a weeping wife and three bairnies."

"Alack," quoth the good old lord, "my heart is sorry for thee; go call Willie, my son, to come speedily. Go call up hastily the men that live by the waterside. They who will not ride for Telfer's cattle, let them never again look me in the face. Call up Wat o'Harden and his sons, call up Borthwick Water, Gaudilands and Allanhaugh, call Gilmanscleugh and Commonside; ride by the gate at Priesthaughswire and call the Currors of the Lee, and call brave Willie of Gorrinberry as ye come down the Hermitage slack."

So the Scotts rode and ran bravely and steadily, shouting "Ride for Branksome," and when Willie looked ahead he saw the cattle being driven fast up the Frostylee brook, and to the plain.

"Who drives yon cattle?" cried Willie Scott, "to make us a laughing stock?" "'Tis I, the Captain of Bewcastle; I will not hide my name from thee."

"Let Telfer's cattle go back, or by the faith of my body," said Willie, "I'll ware my dame's calf-skin on thee."

"I will not let the cattle go back neither for thy love nor fear; I will drive Jamie Telfer's cattle in spite of all your company of Scotts."

"Set on them, lads!" cried Willie; "set on them cruelly; there will be many an empty saddle before they come to Ritterford."

So they set to with heart and hand, and blows fell like hail until many were slain and many a horse ran masterless. But Willie was struck by a sword through the headpiece and fell to the ground, and auld Wat of Harden wept for rage when he saw that his son was slain. He took off his steel cap and waved it thrice, and the snow on the Dinlay mountain was never whiter than the locks of his hair.

"Revenge! revenge!" he cried; "lay on them, lads. Willie's death shall be revenged or we will never see Teviotside again."

The lances flew into splinters, and many another brave rider fell, and before the Kershope ford was reached, the Scots had got the victory. John of Brigham was slain, and John of Barlow, and thirty more of the Captain's men lay bleeding on the ground. The Captain himself was run through the right thigh and the bone broken, and never would woman love him again, if he should live a hundred years.

"Take back the kye!" said he; "they are dear kye to some of us; never will a fair lady smile on me if I should live to be a hundred."

Word came to the Captain's bride in her bower, that her lord had been taken prisoner. "I would rather have had a winding-sheet," said she, "and helped to put it over his head than that he should have been disgraced by the Border Scot when he led his men over Liddel."

There was a wild gallant there named Watty Wudspurs (Madspurs) who cried, "Let us on to his house in Stanegirthside, if any man will ride with us!"

So they came to Stanegirthside, pulled down the trees,

burst open the door, and drove out all the Captain's kye before them.

An old woman of the Captain's kin cried, "Who dare loose the Captain's kye, or answer to him and his men ?"

"It is I, Watty Wudspurs, that loose the kye; I will not hide my name from thee; and I will loose them in spite of him and his men."

When they came to the fair Dodhead they were a welcome sight, for instead of his own ten milk kye Jamie Telfer had now got thirty-three. He paid the rescue shot in gold and silver, and at Willie Scott's burial, there were many weeping eyes.

Chapter XXXVIII

Muckle-mou'd Meg

THE Scott family was very powerful on the Border in the days of Queen Elizabeth, the bravest and strongest of them being the bold Lord of Buccleuch. His name is often mentioned in Border history, and so is that of another Scott, "auld Wat Scott of Harden." He was a fit man for these wild times, being both brave and canny. He married a beautiful Border lass, "the Flower of Yarrow," and it is surprising how many able men have descended from this marriage. Not only did Sir Walter Scott and Robert Louis Stevenson claim descent from this fine old freebooter; his daughter Maggie married Gilbert Elliot of Stobs, nicknamed "Gibbie wi' the Golden Garters," and from them were descended George Augustus Elliot (Lord Heathfield), famous for his splendid defence of Gibraltar, worthy of the best Border traditions, and also the Elliots of Minto, who have twice been Viceroys of India, once late in the eighteenth and once early in the twentieth century.

But on one occasion one of the sons of Scott of Harden came perilously near to finding out how far his neck was capable of carrying the weight of his body. It was late in Queen Elizabeth's reign, and King James VI. of Scotland was extra anxious to live at peace with England, for he expected now very soon to be King over both countries. So he told his Warden, the bold Buccleuch, to restrain the wild Scotch freebooters; and you may imagine that the order was little to their liking. Young Willie Scott, Scott of Harden's son, quickly determined that cattle he must steal anyhow; he was his father's son, and did not his father once say, as he gazed longingly at a fine English haystack, "if only ye'd got four legs, haystack, ye would not be standing there!" So as Willie Scott was forbidden to steal English cattle, he decided to steal Scotch.

Sir Gideon Murray, of Elibank Castle, was an old enemy of the Scott family, having once been told off to punish them for some audacious act of theirs. And Sir Gideon had some cattle that would make any Borderer's mouth water and his arm itch to drive them home. So Willie and a few boon companions started off one night for Elibank. But a warning voice had reached Sir Gideon, and Willie received a warm reception, and was taken prisoner. He lay in the castle dungeon all night, reflecting on the folly of being caught, and fully expecting to be hanged very early next morning, perhaps without even his breakfast to comfort him!

But early on the fatal morning, Lady Murray startled her husband by asking him if he really meant to hang Willie Scott. He looked at her as if she were mad; of course, what else was there to do? Then she unfolded her scheme. She had a very plain-looking daughter known as "Muckle mou'd Meg," or Margaret with the extremely large mouth. Young Scott was handsome and of good family, and poor Meg would never again have such a chance of getting a good husband. Why not release Willie Scott, if only he would marry Muckle-mou'd Meg?

They were men of action in those days, and the priest

was instantly sent for. Then, all being ready, the prisoner was brought forth. He was shown on the one hand the priest and the girl, and on the other hand the tree and the noose, and was asked to take his choice. His first proud feeling was that he would be mocked at if he married such a girl on such terms, and he walked bravely towards the rope. But the nearer he got to it the uglier it looked. He had to confess to himself that it was not at all a comfortable looking rope; he had a nasty feeling round his neck from merely looking at it, and thought it would probably feel worse when it got round his throat. Then he looked at the girl; she certainly was not as beautiful as his mother, the lovely Flower of Yarrow; and a Borderer loved a beautiful wife. But if he hanged he would have no wife at all! Then he suggested that he should have three days to think it over, but Murray said no, neither priest nor noose was prepared to wait, he must decide at once. Then he looked again at Meg and saw a kind glance in her eye; she felt sorry for the handsome young fellow. Then he knew she had a good heart, and that decided the matter; he went up and kissed her with a good grace, and the priest married them straight away.

Afterwards he became Sir William Scott, and an important man on the Border. And, best of all, Meg proved to be a real good wife to him, and he never regretted the day when he elected to suffer the knot to be tied by the priest instead of by the hangman.

Chapter XXXIX

The Dowie Dens of Yarrow

THIS is one of the most famous and widely known of all the Border ballads, and has proved a source of inspiration to several poets, including Wordsworth, who wrote three poems upon the subject. The bard does not relate the full particulars, but gives only the barest outlines of facts, which were well known in his day, and still live in tradition. The story tells of a duel between two brothers-in-law. The very spot where it took place is still pointed out, a low muir on the Yarrow banks. The slain knight was apparently Walter Scott, one of the ancestors of Lord Napier. His murderer was his brother-in-law, John Scott. "Dowie" means melancholy, and "den" is a word used to describe a narrow, rocky valley, usually wildly beautiful.

Late at e'en drinking the wine,
And e'er they paid the lawing,
They set a combat them between,
To fight it in the dawing.[1]

"O stay at home my noble lord,
O stay at home my marrow.
My cruel brother will you betray,
On the dowie houms [2] of Yarrow."

[1] Dawn. [2] Hillocks.

"O fare ye well, my lady gay!
O fare ye well, my Sarah!
For I must go, though I ne'er return
From the dowie banks of Yarrow."

She kissed his cheek, she combed his hair,
As oft she had done before, O,
She belted him with his noble brand,
"And he's away to Yarrow."

As he gaed up the Tennies bank
I wot he gaed with sorrow,
Till down in a den he spied nine armed men,
On the dowie houms of Yarrow.

"O come ye here to part your land,
The bonnie forest thorough?
Or come ye here to wield your brand,
On the dowie houms of Yarrow?"

"I come not here to part my land,
And neither to beg nor borrow,
I come to wield my noble brand
On the bonnie banks of Yarrow.

"If I see all, ye're nine to ane;
And that's an unequal marrow;
Yet will I fight, while lasts my brand,
On the bonnie banks of Yarrow."

Four has he hurt, and five has slain,
On the bloody braes of Yarrow,
Till that stubborn knight came him behind,
And ran his body thorough.

"Gae hame, gae hame, good brother John,
And tell your sister Sarah,

To come and lift her leafu'[1] lord;
He's sleepin' sound on Yarrow."

"Yestreen I dreamed a dolefu' dream,
I fear there will be sorrow!
I dreamed I pu'd the heather green,
Wi' my true love on Yarrow.

"O gentle wind, that bloweth south,
From where my love repaireth,
Convey a kiss from his dear mouth,
And tell me how he fareth!

"But in the glen strive armed men;
They've wrought me dole and sorrow;
They've slain—the comeliest knight they've slain,
He bleeding lies on Yarrow."

As she sped down yon high, high hill,
She gaed wi' dole and sorrow,
And in the den spied ten slain men,
On the dowie banks of Yarrow.

She kissed his cheek, she kaim'd his hair,
She searched his wounds all thorough,
She kiss'd them till her lips grew red,
On the dowie houms of Yarrow.

"Now haud[2] your tongue, my daughter dear,
For a' this breeds but sorrow;
I'll wed ye to a better lord,
Than him ye lost on Yarrow."

"O haud your tongue, my father dear!
Ye mind me but of sorrow;
A fairer rose did never bloom
Than now lies cropp'd on Yarrow."

[1] Lawful. [2] Hold.

"She kissed his cheek, she kaim'd his hair,
She searched his wounds all thorough."

Chapter XL

Belted Will and the Baronry of Gilsland

"When for the lists they sought the plain
The stately lady's silken rein
  Did noble Howard hold;
Unarmed by her side he walk'd
And much, in courteous phrase they talk'd
  Of feats of arms of old.
Costly his garb; his Flemish ruff
Fell o'er his doublet, shaped of buff,
  With satin slashed and lined;
Tawny his boot and gold his spur,
His cloak was all of Poland fur,
  His hose with silver twined.
His Bilboa blade, by Marchmen felt,
Hung in a broad and studded belt;
Hence, in rude phrase, the Borderers still
Call'd noble Howard, *Belted Will*."

SCOTT, *Lay of the Last Minstrel.*

ONE of the many picturesque figures of Border history was "Belted Will," or to call him by his proper name and title, Lord William Howard, a younger son of the powerful Duke of Norfolk.

His mother had died when he was an infant, and his father, the foremost Roman Catholic nobleman in England, took up the cause of Mary Queen of Scots, whom he wished to marry. For this treason against Queen Elizabeth he was beheaded in 1572, when young Lord William was only nine years old. At the age of fourteen the young lord's guardians arranged for him a marriage with Elizabeth Dacre, a member of a powerful Border family, and heiress to the Baronry of Gilsland. As the bride was even younger than her boy-husband, let us hope that they both went to school again immediately after the marriage!

When he grew to manhood, Lord William warmly supported the Roman Catholic cause and was imprisoned by Elizabeth; but when James became King, he was released and restored to his estates on the Border. Throughout the remainder of his career he was the most notable man of his district. He knew how to make himself respected by his wild neighbours. His fame and power were great. He founded the fortunes of his family so surely that he it is who is usually thought of as the ancestor of the Earls of Carlisle, though his great-grandson was the first to hold the title.

Lord William had great energy and many interests, and was remarkable as being an "all-round" man. He was equally a leader of men and a lover of books; no detail in the management of his estates was too small for him to study; he was a good husband to his wife, and a splendid father to his fifteen children. He selected the most beautiful of his several castles, that of Naworth, and repaired and almost rebuilt it; he took there the fine old oak ceiling from the ancient castle of Kirkoswald, which was ornamented with portraits of all the kings of England. Visitors to Naworth can see to-day the "hall of Belted Will," by kind permission of the present Earl of Carlisle.

He was something of a poet and very much of an antiquarian. His estates were full of interesting things, and none knew them better than he. There were miles of the Roman wall, still in excellent condition; there were many Roman altars and inscriptions, which he copied and translated; quite near him, at Coome Crags, was a Roman quarry, which can still be seen to-day, with marks of Roman tools on its stones. It stands in a beautiful wood by the side of the lovely river Irthing. And only a little further on, standing on a fine cliff overlooking the river, is the old Roman station of Amboglanna, a fort that covered five and a half acres, with walls that were once five feet thick, the main foundations of which are still standing, clear enough for anyone to trace them out. It is quieter there to-day than it was in Roman times, or in the stirring days of Belted Will!

It is good to think that this broad-shouldered, gallant, powerful nobleman, who could ride, shoot, fight and keep this wild district in order, was at the same time such a clever student and book-worm. They tell a story that he was once sitting in his library intent on a book when his men brought in a robber whom they had caught red-handed, and asked Lord William to try him. Belted Will, angry at being interrupted, cried out:—"Don't disturb me; hang him!" Half an hour later he rose and came down to try the man, but finding that he was already hanged he went on with his book. It is only fair to add that robbers in those days expected no mercy when caught.

One of the many clever things that Lord William did was to have figures carved in oak to represent soldiers; these he placed on the top of his high towers, and deceived the Scots into thinking that he had a large and very watchful garrison! These figures can still be seen at Naworth.

Near Naworth Castle is Lanercost Priory, where King Edward I. stayed on his way to Scotland. There is a secret passage from Naworth tower which is supposed to run under the river to Lanercost. No one is allowed to go through it, as it is considered dangerous; the people of the district say that the last man to do so was Oliver Cromwell.

Visitors to Naworth to-day should certainly go on to Gilsland itself, the picturesque straggling little town, which was the head of the Baronry which Elizabeth Dacre brought to her boy-husband. The Irthing at Gilsland runs through a wonderfully beautiful gorge, rocky and wooded, wild and romantic. Stand on the venturesome stepping stones near the old church, with the river rushing at your very feet, and see if this is an exaggeration of the beauties of the scene. Right in the midst of the glen you can see the "Popping-stone" where Sir Walter Scott walked with the lady of his choice and asked her to marry him. Readers of "Guy Mannering" can see in Over Denton church near Gilsland the grave of Meg Merrilees, who died here at the age of ninety-eight.

The town is also interesting for the fact that the county border is at Gilsland, and there is an inn so built that it stands in both counties, and contains a bed in which you can sleep with your head in Northumberland and your feet in Cumberland!

There is a story of Belted Will that tells eloquently of the strength of his character. When he was released from prison by King James he found his estates so ruined by careless management that he knew that great care was needed to put things right again; so until he got his affairs into order, all the pocket-money that he would allow himself was twenty shillings per month!

Bold William, Belted Will, gallant Lord Howard, as you will, died at Naworth in 1640 aged seventy-seven, one year after the death of his devoted wife. His descendants were, like himself, students and men of action; the present Earl of Carlisle is directly sprung from him, and is very proud of the fact.

Chapter XLI

Gilderoy

GILDEROY was a celebrated and most daring highwayman, who roamed far, and was well-known all over Scotland and indeed in London. His death inspired a very striking ballad, but this is hardly a Border Lowland ballad, but refers chiefly to another Border district, namely, that between the Lowlands and Highlands. Just as the Scottish Lowlanders thought the English their legitimate quarry, so the Highlanders in turn looked upon the Lowlanders as created to supply them with all they lacked. There is a story on record of a Highland chief who, finding his men had carelessly robbed another Highlander, returned the spoil with a handsome apology, and issued stringent orders that in future nothing was to be taken except in the Lowlands, "where all men make their prey."

Among the robber clans of the Highlands, the MacGregors stand easily in the first rank. In a long series of Scottish Acts of Parliament, they are habitually referred to as "the wicked clan Gregor, so long continuing in blood, slaughter, theft, and robbery." One of their most famous exploits was the battle of Glenfruin, when they defeated their enemies, the Colquhouns, and slew two hundred of them. The Colquhouns appeared before the King at Stirling with the bloody shirts stripped off their dead, and the law was put in motion against the

MacGregors more vigorously than ever. This was in 1603. The execution of Gilderoy, as described in our poem, took place in 1638. His real name was Patrick MacGregor, and the fact that he belonged to this Ishmaelite clan, whose hand was directed against every man, and whose very name had been solemnly abolished, may well serve as an excuse for his career of crime. Gilderoy, in Gaelic, means the red-haired gillie or lad, and besides the name there are many other points of similarity between him and Rob Roy, who was the head of the Clan MacGregor in the following century. Both Gilderoy and Rob Roy were professional blackmailers, that is, they could be relied on never to plunder anyone who was prudent enough to buy them off by paying a fixed contribution. This is what is meant in the following lines of the ballad—

"All these did honestly possess
He never did annoy,
Who never failed to pay their cess
To my love, Gilderoy."

The "cess" is the blackmail, or insurance against robbery. The widespread reputation of Gilderoy is attested by the many legends of him which are printed in the old chap-books and "Lives of the Highwaymen." According to these authorities, Gilderoy once robbed Oliver Cromwell near Glasgow; but an even more romantic episode of his career was a roaming trip upon the continent, in the course of which he is said to have picked Cardinal Richelieu's pocket while he was celebrating mass in the King's presence, at the church of St Denis in Paris. He made his way even to Madrid, where he succeeded in carrying off the Duke of Medina-Celi's plate. Altogether a most notorious and dashing cateran.

The ballad is supposed to be spoken by a young woman who had all her life been attached to him.

"Gilderoy was a bonnie boy,
Had roses to his shoon ;[1]
His stockings were of silken soy,
With garters hanging down.
It was, I ween, a comely sight
To see so trim a boy ;
He was my jo, and heart's delight,
My handsome Gilderoy.

. . . . . .

My Gilderoy and I were born
Both in one town together ;
We scant were seven years before
We 'gan to love each other.
Our daddies and our mammies they
Were filled with meikle joy,
To think upon the bridal day
Of me and Gilderoy."

But there intervened the spirit of adventure which had ever been the birthright of all of his surname,

"Oh, that he still had been content
With me to lead his life !
But ah ! his manful heart was bent
To stir in deeds of strife ;
And he in many a venturous deed
His courage bold would try ;
And now this gars[2] my heart to bleed
For my dear Gilderoy."

No doubt those who knew Gilderoy personally would have agreed, as was actually said of Rob Roy, that he was a benevolent and humane man " in his way."

"My Gilderoy, both far and near,
Was feared in every town ;

[1] Shoes. [2] Makes.

And boldly bore away the gear
Of many a Lowland loun,
For man to man durst meet him none,
He was so brave a boy;
At length with numbers he was ta'en,
My winsome Gilderoy."

He was not so fortunate as Rob Roy, who ultimately died peacefully in his bed. Gilderoy had lost the game, and he had to pay the stakes.

"Of Gilderoy so feared they were,
They bound him fast and strong;
To Edinbro' they led him there,
And on a gallows hung.
They hung him high above the rest,
He was so trim a boy;
There died the youth whom I loved best,
My handsome Gilderoy."

Thus perished one of the characteristic products of an age whose standards were so different from ours that we can hardly judge him fairly. He was banned before his birth, a scion of a race so indomitably and innately ferocious that the law attempted to extirpate them, root and branch. The very name of Gregor could be given by no clergyman at baptism, under penalty of deprivation and banishment. Cunning and politic neighbours were not slow to take advantage of the stubborn disposition of the MacGregors, and gradually stripped them of their once extensive lands in Argyle and Perthshire. Gilderoy might well consider that he was "an honester man than stood on any of their shanks," and we may be excused for feeling a very lively sympathy with him, and for echoing in our inmost hearts the exquisitely feminine point of view expressed by the lady composer of the ballad.

"If Gilderoy had done amiss,
He might have banished been;
Ah! what sore cruelty is this
To hang such handsome men!
To hang the flower of Scottish land,
So sweet and fair a boy!
No lady had so white a hand
As thee, my Gilderoy!

When he had yielded up his breath
I bare his corpse away;
With tears, that trickled for his death,
I washt his comely clay;
And sicker[1] in a grave sae deep
I laid the dear lo'ed boy;
And now for ever maun I weep,
My winsome Gilderoy."

[1] Safely.

Chapter XLII

Archie Armstrong's Oath

"And oft since then, to England's King,
The story he has told ;
And aye, when he 'gan rock and sing,
Charlie his sides would hold."

ARCHIE ARMSTRONG lived in Eskdale, where he did his best to keep up the grand reputation of his family as being among the very boldest sheep-stealers of the Border. His house was at Stubholm, where the Wauchope stream runs into the river Esk, near where the picturesque town of Langholm now stands. Living in the reign of Charles I., after the union of crowns, the profession of freebooter was far less honourable than of old. He could not now plead that he was a Border soldier, fighting against his nation's enemy. The wild Border blood in him might cry out for the old adventurous career, but he could no longer hope for the aid of powerful Border families. When cornered, his sole protector would be his own wits, and woe betide him if they failed !

Archie's house was about eight miles from the Border, and he could not help strolling towards the fascinating line and tasting the sweetness of temptation. When the chance came that seemed to him sufficiently safe, he would go home in company though he had walked out alone ; the " company " being a good fat English sheep.

One night a shepherd had marked him lingering about, and had watched him, and raised an alarm. Away went stout Archie at a Marathon pace; half way home he passed Gilnockie tower, where his ancestor bold Johnie Armstrong lived so gaily. "Alas!" thought Archie, dolefully, "he too was hanged in the end!"

He got home well in front of his pursuers, but his wife gave him small encouragement. With typical Scottish dourness she remarked to him, "Ye will be ta'en this night and hanged i' the morning."

But Archie put a braw face on it, and declared that he would never hang for one silly sheep. Quicker than any butcher he skinned and roughly trimmed the dead animal, throwing the rejected parts into the swift stream. Then rejoicing in the fact that his child was away with its aunt, he put the carcase carefully in the cradle and began rocking it and singing a lullaby to it, as if he were the most loving father in all the British Isles.

The pursuers now rushed in, and began to accuse Archie triumphantly; but he rebuked them for making so much noise, telling them that his child was at death's door! As for stealing their sheep, he took a solemn oath that if he had done such a thing he would ask to be doomed to "eat the flesh this very cradle holds!"

Such an oath on the Borders was a very serious matter; they little knew that the only flesh in the cradle was sheep's flesh, which Archie asked nothing better than to devour!

Impressed but not convinced, his enemies carefully searched the whole of Archie's house and garden; it was only with very great unwillingness that they at last decided that they must miss the supreme pleasure of hanging him! They went away saying that they must have been deluded by the devil or by witches; and the shepherd resolved to hang a branch of rowan-tree (mountain-ash) by his fold, for that was well-known to have the power to keep witches away.

As soon as they were all on their road to England again, Archie skipped about like a dancing fiddler. "Wife," he said, "I never knew before that I would make such a good nurse."

After this Archie wandered down to London, and his wild jests becoming famous, he was made Court Jester by King Charles I. And many a time he acted the story to the King, rocking a pretended cradle, and singing a persuasive lullaby, to the King's intense amusement.

Nevertheless, Archie lost his place by his boldness. These were the days of Archbishop Laud (1637), who was hated by the Scots. One day, as the archbishop was about to say grace before dinner, Archie asked the King's permission to say grace instead. The King consented, and the jester's double-meaning words were as follows :—

"All *praise* to God, and little *laud* to the devil!"

The archbishop, in many senses a little man, had Archie dismissed in disgrace. But, such were the chances of these uncertain times, the archbishop was executed in the end, while the sheepstealer escaped that fate!

Chapter XLIII

Christie's Will

THE resourceful Archie, whose tale we have just told, was not the only one of the reckless Armstrongs to keep up the old freebooting habits in the reign of Charles I. There lived at Gilnockie tower (the old residence of the famous Johnie Armstrong) in the parish of Cannobie, a notorious Willie Armstrong, known as Christie's Will. Like Archie, he more than once owed his life to his ready wit. He was shut up in Jedburgh jail when the Earl of Traquair, Lord High Treasurer, paid the prison an official visit. When he asked Will the cause of his being there, the freebooter answered :—

" For stealing two halters, my lord."

Traquair was surprised, but Will afterwards owned that there was a fine colt at the end of each halter.

Traquair was amused and pleased by the boldness of the man, and had him set free.

Some little time afterwards Traquair was involved in a law-suit which was set down to be decided by Lord Durie, who seems to have let it be known before-hand what his opinion was upon the case. Nothing would save Traquair's interests except that Durie must be got out of the way before the case began. But how was it to be done ?

Christie's Will was appealed to, and merely said "Leave it to me."

It was the judge's habit to take horseback exercise on the sands of Leith without any attendant. One morning, whilst so riding, a well-dressed and gentlemanly stranger, on a good horse, happened to overtake him; a courteous greeting led to a friendly conversation, in which the stranger proved himself so affable and entertaining that the judge rode on by his side without suspicion. Suddenly, when they had come to a lonely spot, Lord Durie found himself seized by this muscular gentleman, smothered up in a big cloak, whisked off his horse and on to the stranger's, who galloped off, mischief knows where! It was Christie's Will, carrying out his promise.

The judge's horse galloped home, riderless. Search was made, but the judge could not be found. It could only be supposed that he had been thrown off into the sea. His successor was appointed, and Lord Traquair's case was heard and won!

Lord Durie had languished for several months in a dreary underground vault. I wonder if he thought of the many poor wretches he had sentenced to a similar fate? Suddenly at midnight he was roughly awakened, muffled up as before, and carried away again by his captor on horseback. Next morning, by the light of the newly-risen sun, he found himself on the very spot by the sands of Leith from which he had been kidnapped! We will hope that every one, including his successor, was glad when he thus came to life again.

When the Civil War began, the Earl of Traquair was faithful to King Charles I. Having some papers of importance that he wished to have given into the King's own hands, he entrusted these to the bold freebooter. Christie's Will did his errand, and received an equally important answer. But spies at Court had given Cromwell word of the matter, and the command was sent up to Carlisle that Will Armstrong must be intercepted there. Not knowing his danger, Will halted in the town to refresh his horse, then pushed forward to the bridge which crossed the Eden on the Northern boundary of the city. Cromwell's soldiers were waiting for him; the bridge was high and narrow, the broad Eden waters were swirling in high flood.

Christie's Will, without one second's hesitation, spurred his horse over the parapet. He sank . . . he came up . . . he sank . . . he came up . . . he sank . . . he came up, this time at the very bank. He cut his heavy, dripping cloak from his shoulders; relieved of the weight, his horse struggled to the land. Away went Will, away went the troopers after him. It was a hard race to the river Esk, and this also Will had to swim. But now he was in Scotland, and his friends were at hand; gaily Will turned to his pursuers, who dared not cross the water; " Good friends," cried he, " come over and drink with me ! " But they showed him their backs, and their horses's tails, and he saw no more of them.

Such were the exploits of Christie's Will; he was the last of the free-booters, but he certainly knew how to live up to their boldest traditions.

Chapter XLIV

Northumberland at the time of the Civil War

DURING the stormy days of King Charles I., the Borders, and especially Northumberland, saw many stirring scenes. It must be remembered that shortly before the Long Parliament was elected, King Charles almost came to war with the Scottish Presbyterians, because they would not obey the harsh rule of Archbishop Laud. The Scots raised an army under the lead of shrewd general Alexander Leslie, the "old, little, crooked soldier," of great experience, trained by the great Gustavus of Sweden. In 1639 Charles sent ships up to the Forth, in reply to which Leslie marched his army to threaten the border. The old quarrel between the two countries began to blaze up again. King Charles led an army to the border and was received with splendid applause at Newcastle. Many joined his army, and shouted with joy at the thought of meeting the Scots in battle. But they were an untrained disorderly crew, who fired their guns off at random and kept no military order whatever. Gallant Leslie marched his men down to Duns Law, in South Berwickshire, and was ready to fight. But King Charles would not trust his army that length; he made terms with his opponents, promising them the reforms they set their hearts upon, and the two armies melted away like school-boys at the end of the term.

Things were soon as bad as before. Lord Conway was sent by the King to put Newcastle into a strong defensive state. His greatest difficulty was to get money for the purpose, for the King's quarrel with his various Parliaments had deprived him of supplies. The badly paid troops mutinied, and the ring-leader was shot. Very soon the Scottish army came across the Tweed, the Highlanders armed with bows and arrows.

They pitched their camp on Heddon Law, and soon proved to the country folk that they had not come for plunder, but would pay for all they wanted to eat. This re-assured the country people, who had no real quarrel with the Scots, and even became most friendly to them.

With Lord Conway it was otherwise; he was the King's officer, and was bound to offer resistance. His opinion was that if once the Scots crossed the Tyne, and attacked Newcastle from the south or Gateshead side, they were sure of victory. Accordingly, leaving a strong garrison to protect the town, he marched out with two thousand or more foot and fully one thousand horse to command the important ford across the Tyne at Newburn, a place five or six miles due west of Newcastle. It is interesting to remember that here also the Romans had had fortifications, along the line of the wall, and the very spot where the Scots and English fought may well have been the scene of contests between the Roman Legions and the wild Picts.

The English arrived first, on the south bank of the river, and threw up earth-works hastily. Very soon they saw the Scots march into Newburn village, on the north bank, where they employed themselves by hauling their cannon up to the church tower. Remarkable cannon they were, made out of bar-iron hooped together with cord and wet, raw hides! But they were not required to carry any distance, the foe was only on the other side of the Tyne. All the morning the enemies looked at one another across the river, each hesitating to fire the first shot of the war. At last an English officer shot a Scotch officer, and the fight began. The Scots were on the higher ground, and their cannon, rough as they were, sent heavy shot on to the English. Then when the river tide went down, the Scots rushed across the ford, and the battle was soon won, the royal standard being taken. English runaways rushed through the woods and into Newcastle, crying, "Fly for your lives, naked devils have destroyed us!" Whether they referred to kilted Highlanders is uncertain. Anyway, Leslie and his Scots entered Newcastle in triumph, but were afterwards bought off with a payment of £60,000 and recrossed the Tweed into Scotland.

This was in 1641, a year in which King Charles was quarrelling bitterly with his Long Parliament, though the actual civil war in England did not begin till 1642. Early in 1642 it was decided that so important a town as Newcastle ought to be put in a stronger state of defence.

William Cavendish, Earl of Newcastle, was made governor of the town, but he was much hindered in his plans by lack of money. King Charles, however, promoted him from Earl to Marquis of Newcastle, and the lack of funds he made up as best he was able. However, the Governor of Holy Island, off the Northumberland shore, found himself left for sixteen months without any pay! He wrote to the King's treasury a protest in verse, beginning:—

R *The Storming of Newcastle*

"The great commander of the Cormorants,
The geese and ganders of these hallowed lands,
Where Lindisfarne and Holy Island stands,
These worthless lines sends to your worthy hands."

The allusion in the first two lines is to the fact that Holy Island and the Farne Islands were then, and are still to-day, so thinly peopled that sea-birds gather there in large numbers, adding greatly to the wild beauties of these islets and rocks.

In January 1644 a serious struggle began. Leslie and his soldiers crossed the Tweed at Berwick bridge and again entered Northumberland. General Bayly marched his men from Kelso across the frozen river and joined Leslie at Alnwick. Warkworth Castle, though it contained cannon and provisions, surrendered at once. The Scottish general gravely told Bemerton, the governor, that if he had learnt to fight as well as he had learnt to dance his castle could never have been taken! The country districts of Northumberland had no quarrel with the Scots, and it was soon evident that the real fight would be at Newcastle, bravely held by the Marquis and by the Mayor, Sir John Marley.

The Scottish "murthering pieces," as the cannon were called, were brought down by sea, and the obstinate conflict began. Despite the terrible weather of a very rough February, frequent skirmishes took place, while the Scots closed nearer and nearer round the gallantly defended town. Leslie soon found that the defences had been put into good order; the ditch round the town was dug deep, and close to the walls; the walls themselves were strongly underpinned. The battlements were strengthened by stone and lime, but the top stones were loosened so as to slip if the enemy attempted to mount them. Every cannon was placed carefully, to the best advantage.

But the Marquis of Newcastle was called southward by the needs of his King. With him were his thousand brave "White coats," so called because they wore white coats which they promised to dye in the blood of the enemy. But they met the terrible Ironsides at Marston Moor, and in a conflict of furious bravery on both sides, all of the gallant thousand except thirty were slain on the field of battle.

This was in July of 1644, but it did not affect the siege of Newcastle, which still dragged obstinately on, under the skilful guidance of the dauntless Mayor. By October, Sir John Marley was so buoyed up by his success that he sent a letter to General Leslie to ask if he was still alive! This the Scots took to be an insult, and a grand assault was begun. The Scots were furious, and the defence was desperate. The roar of the cannon and the rattle of the musketry were succeeded, as the assault got nearer and nearer to its aim, by the clashing of swords and the clanging of pikes. At last, the regiments of Loudoun and Buccleugh succeeded in forcing their way into the town. In vain the defenders made their last gallant charge; their cause was now hopeless, and soon the market-place was filled with fugitives, who flung down their arms and cried aloud for quarter at the hands of the triumphant Scots.

In these days the defender was often made to feel the anger of the victors, who in the flush and cruelty of victory avenged their dead, only too terribly, upon the losing side. Not so at Newcastle. Prominent in its day, it stands out because of the mercy of the Scottish conquerors as much as for the heroism of its defence. In this, the last great struggle on English ground between Scots and English, it is pleasing indeed to recall facts that redound to the high honour of both parties.

Chapter XLV

Montrose and Lesly

JAMES GRAHAM, the great Marquis of Montrose who at first sided with the Scottish Covenanters against Charles I., was so out of sympathy with the extreme turn which affairs took later against that unhappy monarch that he went over to the King's side. Gathering the Highland Clans under his standard, he marched Southward and defeated the Covenanters in a series of brilliantly fought battles. He occupied Edinburgh, and laid great plans to complete the conquest of Scotland by subduing the Borderland.

If the Borders had remained in their old fighting state no doubt many a Border chief would have joined Montrose's army and aided his bold plans. But, unfortunately for King Charles, the Borders had been tamed and disarmed since the union of England and Scotland under James I. Only a few adventurous spirits like Christie's Will remained as examples of the old wild days.

The remnant of the army of the Covenanters was commanded by the stern General David Lesly (not the Alexander Leslie who figures in the preceding chapter), and was somewhere in the Border district. Gay Gallant Montrose did not bother as to exactly where this army was; he despised it too heartily. He himself was at Selkirk, while his army was encamped on the neighbouring plain of Philiphaugh.

Montrose was busy writing a cheering message to King Charles to the effect that he had now no enemy left in Scotland who could offer an effective resistance to his arms. Little did he think that General Lesly was gradually creeping nearer, nearer, and was now actually within four miles of his army. With the advantage of a thick Scotch mist, Lesly's men actually burst upon Montrose's infantry without a single scout having seen them to give warning of their approach! In such confusion, Montrose's men had no chance whatever.

The Marquis galloped up, only to find his soldiers hopelessly defeated and great numbers slain. There was nothing left but for those to escape who could. The Marquis succeeded in cutting his way through, and gathered his troops to fight again later on; but his efforts were doomed to failure.

A popular ditty of these days, sung to a stirring tune, was called "Lesly's March." Sir Walter Scott seems to regard this as wholly serious, and ranks it as a Covenanter song. It appears to me, however, that many of the lines have a very sarcastic flavour; no doubt the Covenanters did really think that

> "There's none in the right but we,
> Of the old Scottish nation";

but they would probably have phrased it a little less baldly. To me it appears as if this song were the work of an onlooker and not a partisan; one ready to see the faults of both sides, and very much inclined to hold back his final opinion till he saw which was going to win. But let the March speak for itself.

LESLY'S MARCH

March ! march :
Why the de'il do ye na march ?
Stand to your arms, my lads,
Fight in good order ;
Front about, ye musketeers all,
Till ye come to the English Border ;
  Stand till 't, and fight like men,
  True gospel to maintain.
The parliament's blythe to see us a' coming !
  When to the kirk we come,
  We'll purge it ilka room,
Frae popish relics, and a' sic innovation,
  That a' the world may see,
  There's nane in the right but we,
Of the auld Scottish nation.

A truly partisan ballad of the day describes the battle of Philiphaugh and exults in the defeat of Montrose, " our cruel enemy," it calls him. As a ballad it has no great poetic merit ; the very sober Covenanters probably regarded ballad-making as a frivolity. But it describes rather graphically how an " aged father," from the country-side, led Lesly's army very cautiously and wisely to the very tents of the foe. These details are no doubt accurate ; though the ballad-writer (whoever he was) displays his ignorance of other matters by making the old soldier say that he was at the battle of Solway Moss (which took place one hundred years before) and at that of Dunbar, which was not fought till five years later !

The following are the opening verses of the ballad, giving an idea of its plain, straightforward style :—

On Philiphaugh a fray began,
  At Hairhead-wood it ended;
The Scots out o'er the Græmes they ran,
  Sae merrily they bended;

Sir David frae the Border came,
  Wi' heart an' hand came he;
Wi' him three thousand bonny Scots,
  To bear him company.

Wi' him three thousand valiant men,
  A noble sight to see!
A cloud o' mist them weel conceal'd,
  As close as e'er might be.

When they came to the Shaw burn,
  Said he, "Sae weel we frame,
I think it is convenient
  That we should sing a psalm."

It is not necessary to quote more of it, but it may be remarked that in place of the last line as given here, the *unregenerate* substituted,

"That we should take a dram."

In point of actual fact, *both* versions are probably true!

Chapter XLVI

The Death of Montrose

DURING the imprisonment of King Charles I., at a time when active war on his behalf might do the unhappy monarch more harm than good, the gallant Montrose had retired to France. His bright military fame, his courteous manners, and manly bearing made him friends everywhere, and when he visited Germany the Emperor conferred on him the rank of Marshal. Hearing of the execution of Charles I., Montrose at once placed himself at the disposal of Charles II., now a fugitive in Holland. This prince named him Captain General of Scotland, and the daring hero set out for the Orkney Islands with about five hundred paid soldiers, mostly adventurous Germans and Dutchmen. Only a reckless spirit like Montrose would have undertaken so wild a commission.

Scotland was heartily sick of war, and learnt with consternation of the arrival of this firebrand. Lesly was sent forward with four thousand men to attack Montrose's five hundred! Colonel Strachan led the advanced guard, which fell unexpectedly upon the invading army, and, after a brief, fierce struggle, totally defeated it.

Montrose, disguised as a peasant, entrusted his life to one he believed to be his friend, M'Leod, Laird of Assaint. But this unworthy man betrayed him to his bitterest enemy, General Lesly. Thus, at last, this brilliant commander was in the hands of the bitter Covenanters, into whose hearts his brilliant victories had once spread such terror. Their treatment of him is a black stain upon their memory. For days he was led about in the peasant's disguise, which he had put on; he was carted through the streets of Edinburgh, accompanied by such insults that the populace cried shame upon his captors.

When tried before the Scottish Parliament for treason, he made a most eloquent defence, one of the most notable of his assertions being that he had never stained his victories by slaughtering his foes in cold blood after the battle. In this he was far above his enemies, who had disgraced their victory of Philiphaugh by many an execution, and who were now bent upon taking the life of Montrose himself. The sentence against him was probably decided before his defence had been heard; it ran thus:—

"That James Graham should next day be carried to Edinburgh cross and there hanged on a gibbet 30 feet high for the space of three hours; then to be taken down, his head to be struck off on a scaffold and affixed to the prison; his arms and legs to be stuck up on the four chief towns of the Kingdom, his body to be buried in the place set aside for common criminals."

To this sentence the great Marquis haughtily replied that he would rather have his head so placed than his picture in the King's bedchamber, and that he wished he had limbs enough to be dispersed into all the cities of Christendom, to prove his dying attachment to his king. And in the one evening of life that still remained to him, this accomplished and fearless nobleman employed his time in turning these loyal sentiments into verse.

Despite the fact that he triumphed undaunted over all

the mean inventions of their malice, his enemies persisted to the end.

The executioner tied mockingly round his neck the book that had been published describing his victories; Montrose thanked him, saying that he wore it with more pride than he had ever worn the garter of honour. He uttered a short prayer; then asking them what more indignities they had prepared for him, he patiently and with unbroken spirit yielded his life to the hangman, at the too early age of thirty-eight.

Whatever opinions we may have as to the rights and wrongs of the quarrel, this brutal killing of a gallant soldier and accomplished gentleman can only rank as a hideous blot upon all concerned in it. Every insult hurled at Montrose has returned in the verdict of time with redoubled force against the malice of those who stooped to such vindictiveness. The execution of a soldier who has violated no rule of war is at any time a thing that revolts the human conscience, and a sentence hoarse with the vile taunts of its utterers has so far lost all semblance of justice that it is needless to argue upon it.

In the verdict of history, the great Marquis of Montrose, whether right or wrong in his political views, lived and died like a man of honour.

The ballad of the "Gallant Grahams," written about this time, reflects very sincerely and touchingly the devotion and affection surrounding the great Marquis, accompanied by the very Scottish feeling that in addition to his own personal power and genius, he was also the head of the great Border family of Grahams.

THE GALLANT GRAHAMS

Now, fare thee well, sweet Ennerdale![1]
  Baith kith and countrie I bid adieu;
For I maun away, and I may not stay,
  To some uncouth land which I never knew.

To wear the blue I think it best,
  Of all the colours that I see;
And I'll wear it for the gallant Grahams,
  That are banished from their countrie.

I have no gold, I have no land,
  I have no pearl nor precious stane;
But I wald sell my silken snood,
  To see the gallant Grahams come hame.

In Wallace days, when they began,
  Sir John the Graham[2] did bear the gree
Through all the lands of Scotland wide:
  He was lord of the south countrie.

And so was seen full many a time;
  For the summer flowers did never spring,
But every Graham, in armour bright,
  Would then appear before the king.

They were all drest in armour sheen,
  Upon the pleasant banks of Tay;
Before a king they might be seen,
  These gallant Grahams in their array.

[1] A corruption of Endrickdale. The principal and most ancient possessions of the Montrose family lie along the water of Endrick, in Dumbartonshire.

[2] The faithful friend and adherent of the immortal Wallace slain at the battle of Falkirk.

At the Goukhead our camp we set,
Our leaguer down there for to lay;
And, in the bonny summer light,
We rode our white horse and our gray.

Our false commander sold our king,
Unto his deadly enemie,
Who was the traitor, Cromwell, then;
So I care not what they do with me.

They have betray'd our noble prince,
And banished him from his royal crown;
But the gallant Grahams have ta'en in hand
For to command those traitors down.

In Glen-Prosen [1] we rendezvous'd,
March'd to Glenshie by night and day,
And took the town of Aberdeen,
And met the Campbells in their array.

Five thousand men, in armour strong,
Did meet the gallant Grahams that day
At Inverlochie, where war began,
And scarce two thousand men were they.

Gallant Montrose, that chieftan bold,
Courageous in the best degree,
Did for the king fight well that day;—
The Lord preserve his majestie!

[1] Glen-Prosen is in Angusshire, usually called Forfarshire. The Glenshee road, over the Grampians, is the highest road in Great Britain.

Then woe to Strachan, and Hacket baith!
  And, Lesly, ill death may thou die!
For ye have betray'd the gallant Grahams,
  Who aye were true to majestie.

And the Laird of Assaint has seized Montrose,
  And had him into Edinburgh town;
And frae his body taken the head,
  And quarter'd him upon a trone,

And Huntly's [1] gone the self-same way,
  And our noble king is also gone;
He suffer'd death for our nation,
  Our mourning tears can ne'er be done.

But our brave young king is now come home,
  King Charles the Second in degree;
The Lord send peace into his time,
  And God preserve his majestie!

The ballad-writer's reference to the "coming home" of Charles II. probably means his signing of the Covenant and placing himself entirely at the mercy of the violent bigots who had killed his most faithful servant, Montrose. To this was Charles reduced by the desperate nature of his fortunes. But this course of action entirely severed the Scottish Covenanters from the English Puritans, and admirers of the gallant Montrose can take a grim pleasure in the fact that his arch-enemy, General Lesly, was most disastrously defeated by Cromwell at the battle of Dunbar.

[1] The Marquis of Huntly, one of the few Scottish nobles who never wavered in his devotion to King Charles I., was beheaded by the sentence of the Parliament of Scotland.

Chapter XLVII

The Borderers and the Jacobites

DURING the Jacobite Rising, many of the Border chiefs took up arms in the Stuart cause. Two of these, Lord Derwentwater and Viscount Kenmure, were beheaded on Tower Hill for their part in the unsuccessful rising of 1715, and another, Lord Nithsdale, was only saved from the same fate by the courage of his wife.

This brave woman travelled in the depth of winter from Scotland, but when she reached York the snow was so deep that the stage coach could go no further. She continued her journey alone, though the snow was above the horse's knees, and by good luck she reached London and the Tower in safety, where, by bribing the guards, she managed to see her husband.

She then resolved to petition the King for his life, and she herself tells in a letter to her sister how she waited in the ante-room to see the King (George I.), and how she threw herself at his feet to present the petition. The King tried to get away from her, but she seized hold of his coat, and was dragged on her knees along the floor. This scene produced no result, and as other efforts to procure Nithsdale's release also failed, the Countess determined to save him by a stratagem. She again bribed the guards to let her in, telling them she had joyful news for her husband about the petition. She dressed him in woman's clothes, which she had smuggled in for the occasion, and painted his face, and brought him out, speaking to him as to the woman friend who had accompanied her, but who had already left the prison, calling him "Mrs Betty," and asking him for the love of God to go as quickly as he could to her lodging and fetch her maid, as she wished to go and present her final petition for the release.

All went well, and Nithsdale escaped to France; but the King was highly incensed and declared that the Countess cost him more trouble than any woman in Europe.

Her adventures were not yet over, however. In spite of the fact that the King had wished for her arrest, she travelled to Scotland to fetch her son, and the valuable papers which she had taken the precaution to bury underground on her departure for London.

She was successful in this second journey, and, after concealing herself and her son, until no further search was made for them, this noble and enterprising woman escaped to France and joined her husband. They afterwards went to Rome, where they lived happily for many years.

In an old ballad called "Lord Nithsdale's Dream," he is described as dreaming in the Tower the night before his execution, after having said farewell to his beloved wife.

> "Farewell to thee, Winifred, pride of thy kind,
> Sole ray in my darkness, sole joy in my pain."

He listens for the last sound of her footfall, and catches the last glimpse of her robe at the door, and then all joy and gladness depart out of his life, and he prays alone in his dungeon, thinking of the dreadful dawn that awaits him.

He falls asleep and dreams that he is a frolicsome boy

S "'Tis I, 'tis thy Winifred!"

again, playing amongst the bracken on the braes of the Nith, bathing in its waters and treading joyfully the green heather. Or again he is riding to the hunt on his gallant grey steed, with a plume in his bonnet and a star on his breast, chasing the red deer and the wild mountain roe.

The vision changes, and he dreams that he is telling his love to Winifred, and swearing to be faithful to her, watching the red blushes rise on her cheeks at his words of love, and hearing her sweet voice replying.

Again he is riding at the head of his gallant band.

> "For the pibroch was heard on the hills far away,
> And the clans were all gathered from mountain and glen.
> For the darling of Scotland, their exile adored,
> They raised the loud slogan—they rushed to the strife;
> Unfurl'd was the banner, unsheathed was the sword,
> For the cause of their heart, that was dearer than life."

And now the darksome morn has come, the priest is standing by his side, saying the prayers for the dead. He hears the muffled drum and the bells tolling his death knell; the block is prepared, the headsman comes; and the victim is led bare-headed from his cell.

Waking, he turns on his straw pallet, and sees, by the pale, misty light of a taper, the form of his wife.

> "'Tis I, 'tis thy Winifred!" softly she said,
> "Arouse thee and follow, be bold, never fear,
> There was danger ahead, but my errand has sped,
> I promised to save thee, and lo! I am here!"

Then she puts woman's garb upon him, and together they pass the unsuspecting guards and weary sentinels.

. . . . .

When the peasantry on the Nithsdale estates heard of their Lord's escape their joy was unbounded.

One of the songs published and sung everywhere at the time, begins :—

> " What news to me, carlin'?
> What news to me?"
> " What news!" quo' the carlin',
> The best that God can gie."

The speaker asks if the true king has come to his own, and the carlin' answers.

> " Our ain Lord Nithsdale
> Will soon be 'mang us here.

Then the speaker says :—

> " Brush me my coat, carlin',
> Brush me my shoon;
> I'll awa and meet Lord Nithsdale,
> When he comes to our town.'

" Alack-a-day," says the carlin'. " He has escaped to France, with scarce a penny."

" Then," says the first speaker, " we'll sell our corn and everything we have and send the money to our lord, and we'll make the pipers blow and lads and maidens dance, and we'll all be glad and joyful and play 'The Stuarts back again,' and make the Whigs go mad."

. . . . .

Lord Derwentwater's fate was not so happy as that of Lord Nithsdale, though Lady Derwentwater made a desperate effort to save him.

It was she indeed who had urged him to throw in his lot with the Stuarts, saying that it was not good that he should hide his head when other gentlemen were mustering for the cause.

The peasantry still think that Lady Derwentwater sits on her ruined tower lamenting the evil counsel she gave her husband, and they hasten by in fear when they see her lamp-light flickering.

Derwentwater is described in the old ballads, as "a bonny lord," with hair of gold, and kind love dwelling in his hawk-like eyes.

He passionately loved his beautiful home in Tynedale, the foundations of which may still be seen. The wooded glen below the castle, with the little burn running through it, spanned by a grey bridge is romantically beautiful.

His "Farewell" to all this beauty is pathetic.

"Farewell to pleasant Ditson Hall,
My father's ancient seat;
A stranger now must call thee his,
Which gars [1] my heart to greet. [2]
Farewell each kindly well-known face,
My heart has held so dear:
My tenants now must leave their lands,
Or hold their lives in fear.

No more along the banks of Tyne,
I'll rove in autumn grey;
No more I'll hear, at early dawn,
The lav'rocks [3] wake the day:
Then fare thee well, brave Witherington,
And Forster ever true.
Dear Shaftsbury and Errington,
Receive my last adieu.

And fare thee well, George Collingwood,
Since fate has put us down,
If thou and I have lost our lives,
Our King has lost his crown.
Farewell, farewell, my lady dear,
Ill, ill thou counsell'dst me:
I never more may see thy babe
That smiles upon thy knee.

[1] makes. [2] weep. [3] larks.

And fare thee well, my bonny grey steed,
  That carried me aye so free ;
I wish I had been asleep in my bed,
  The last time I mounted thee.
The warning bell now bids me cease ;
  My troubles nearly o'er ;
Yon sun that rises from the sea,
  Shall rise on me no more.

Albeit that here in London town
  It is my fate to die,
O carry me to Northumberland,
  In my father's grave to lie :
There chant my solemn requiem
  In Hexham's holy towers,
And let six maids of fair Tynedale
  Scatter my grave with flowers.

And when the head that wears the crown,
  Shall be laid low like mine,
Some honest hearts may then lament
  For Radcliff's fallen line.
Farewell to pleasant Ditson Hall,
  My father's ancient seat ;
A stranger now must call thee his,
  Which gars my heart to greet."

Before his death, Earl Derwentwater signed a paper acknowledging "King James the Third" as his sovereign, and saying that he hoped his death would contribute to the service of his King.

He is said to have looked closely at the block, and to have asked the executioner to chip off a rough place that might hurt his neck. Then, pulling off his coat and waistcoat, he tried if the block would fit his head, and told the executioner that when he had repeated "Lord Jesus receive my soul" for the third time, he was to do his office, which the executioner accordingly did at one blow.

History tells that Derwentwater was brave and open-hearted and generous, and that his fate drew tears from the spectators, and was a great misfortune to his country. He was kind to the people on his estates, to the poor, the widow and the orphan.

His request to be buried with his ancestors was refused, and he was interred at St Giles, Holborn, but his corpse was afterwards removed and carried secretly to Northumberland, where it was deposited in Dilston Chapel. The aurora borealis, which appeared remarkably vivid on the night of his execution, was long called in that part of the country " Lord Derwentwater's Lights."

Immediately after Derwentwater's execution, Lord Kenmure also suffered death. After his execution, a letter was found in his pocket addressed to the Pretender, by the title of King James, saying that he died in his faithful service, and asking him to provide for his wife and children.

The following ballad describes his rising in the Stuart cause—

" O Kenmure's on and awa', Willie,
  O Kenmure's on and awa';
And Kenmure's lord's the bravest lord
  That ever Galloway saw.
Success to Kenmure's band, Willie!
  Success to Kenmure's band!
There's no a heart that fears a Whig,
  That rides by Kenmure's hand.

His lady's cheek was red, Willie,
  His lady's cheek was red,
When she saw his steely jupes [1] put on,
  Which smell'd o' deadly feud.

[1] armour.

Here's Kenmure's health in wine, Willie,
Here's Kenmure's health in wine;
There ne'er was a coward o' Kenmure's blude,
Nor yet o' Gordon's line.

There's a rose in Kenmure's cap, Willie,
There's a rose in Kenmure's cap,
He'll steep it red in ruddie heart's blude,
Afore the battle drap.
Here's him that's far awa', Willie,
Here's him that's far awa',
And here's the flower that I lo'e best,
The rose that's like the snaw.

O Kenmure's lads are men, Willie,
O Kenmure's lads are men,
Their hearts and swords are metal true,
And that their foes shall ken.
They'll live, or die wi' fame, Willie,
They'll live, or die wi' fame,
And soon wi' sound o' victorie
May Kenmure's lord come hame.[a]

Chapter XLVIII

The Nine Nicks o' Thirlwall

IF you stand upon Rose Hill, which rises from the banks of the river Irthing just where Northumberland meets Cumberland, you have lying around you one of the finest wild prospects in the United Kingdom. Hills to the north, stretching away into Scotland; hills to the east, broken into picturesque valleys, especially the great gap through which rushes the young Tyne; hills to the south, dominated by the powerful head of Cross Fell, a great sprawling mountain, not a peaked one, the highest stretch of which is nearly three thousand feet above sea level.

But while drinking in the glories of the distances, the eye will note with curiosity a strange-looking but picturesque hill only a couple of miles to the South-east, with a long rocky ridge at its top deeply cut into or "nicked" in nine different places, this giving it a very wild appearance. It is one of these hills which tempts the keen observer to go on and explore it. If we cut direct to it, over the fields, it is rough going, but the view is good all the way. And there are four special objects of interest, all close together; the rushing Tipalt river, Thirlwall Castle, the Roman wall, and the Nine Nicks.

Thirlwall Castle rises tall, square, and stern, with a dark fir-wood behind it at the foot of the hill, where a bend in the rivet makes a natural moat. Approaching it from Rose Hill, it looks as if the building were still nearly complete, but the south side has almost entirely fallen away and all the floors and the roof are out. Edward I. slept in this Castle when it was newly built, in 1306; but now it is grass-grown and moss-grown, and its three bare walls rise gaunt and grim to the sky. It is entirely built out of stones with Roman chisel marks, taken from the great Roman wall, which unfortunately was once regarded as a handy stone-quarry for anyone to take from.

The name "Thirlwall" means "Drill-wall," and marks the spot as that at which the wild Northern tribes first "drilled" or broke through the wall. The name was, of course, given to the place long before this castle was built.

To mount from Thirlwall Castle to the top of the Nine Nicks is an easy enough task for any vigorous person. It is just a fine healthy scramble. When at the top, it becomes evident that some sort of fortification once existed there. In point of fact this was the important Roman station called "Magna" which stood at about the middle of the Roman Wall. The wall ran from sea to sea, that is to say, from the mouth of the Tyne to the Solway. Thus it was nearly eighty miles long, and a very elaborate structure indeed.

It consisted of three distinct portions :—

1. The main stone wall, with a ditch to the north of it.

2. An earth-work to the south of this, consisting of either two or three ramparts about seventy feet apart, with a ditch between.

3. Stations, Castles and Watch-towers. Sometimes these were to the north of the wall, sometimes in the

middle, sometimes south, according to the nature of the country.

The height of the main wall was from sixteen to twenty feet, including battlements. It was six to nine feet thick. Fancy a powerful military wall of about eighteen feet high stretching nearly eighty miles right across England! It hardly seems possible that the Romans could undertake such a work. The square strong stones were carefully selected and often brought from quarries at a distance. These stones flanked the outsides of the wall, and in between was strong concrete which was poured in while in liquid.

The second wall was of earth and stones, and, of course, lower than the first. Then there was a castle every mile, some of which can still be clearly traced, and a "station," about every four miles, of which several interesting ruins remain. There was a road eighteen feet wide between the two walls.

Those who have the energy to toil on for a full dozen miles of rough walking, along the wall, eastward from Thirlwall, will be rewarded by some of the most romantic scenes in Britain. They will see the wall at its best. They will pass Whinshields, the highest point in the wall, 1230 feet above sea level. The wild Northumbrian lakes will lie at their feet; if the day is fine, the Solway will be seen glistening, thirty miles to the west; and on the east the eye follows the Tyne almost to the sea. The Pennine Ridge bars the view twenty miles to the south, while on the North the High Cheviot is clear and strong, thirty miles away.

Passing Whinshields, it is not far to Borcovicus (often called Housteads) where lie the remains of a large Roman Station, wonderful remains, showing the whole outline with startling clearness. This station covered five acres, and here was quartered a cohort of the Tungrian infantry, consisting of a thousand brave soldiers, servants of Imperial Rome.

But, after all, nothing is so impressive as the remains of the wall itself. Stand at the top either of Whinshields or of the Nine Nicks, and try to imagine what it looked like in Roman days. Eastward along the Tyne valley and westward along the Irthing valley ran this wonderful work, this powerful girdle of stone. The very spot was chosen with great judgment, for these valleys gave the Romans a district protected by the bleak hills, where they could live and where they could keep cattle and grow grain. But the hilly nature of the ground must have added to the difficulty of the builders. The wall had to run up steep hill sides and cling to the edge of cliffs, and precipices; it had to be carried by bridges over roaring torrents, and when it reached low-lying ground it had to avoid the treacherous swamps and morasses. And yet, despite every obstacle, the great wall ran on its direct way, as strong and persistent as the great people who built it.

It withstood the shock of war, it was not flung down by soldiers marching against it. But to the people who wanted to build castles or houses or farms, or even to mend roads, the wall offered a mass of material ready to hand, and it suffered not from man's energy so much as from his laziness. Century after century it was robbed of its stones; to-day a series of long grass-grown mounds, a few feet high, running across the meadows, are nearly all that remain of one of the most wonderful pieces of building that was ever erected in Great Britain. Even to-day, in its decay, it is one of the most romantic features of a highly romantic district.

Chapter XLIX

In Wild Northumberland To-day

THESE tales of the Borders would hardly be complete without a few concluding words about the great romantic charm which still invests the Borderline. Let us, for example, make a brief survey of some of the haunting spots in wild Northumberland. We will pass over such towns as Warkworth, Alnwick, Alnmouth ; beautiful as they are, they have moved with the times and are too modern to be more than mentioned here. But in a place like Holy Island we feel the call of the old days, and the charm that was theirs. This Island was the scene of the first efforts of Christianity to curb the wild and warlike Northumbrians ; St Aidan, and St Cuthbert, both men of remarkable genius and great influence, taught there lessons of peace and justice without which every warlike state would decend into mere savagery. The island is about two miles square, and at low tide it is easy to walk across the sands to or from the mainland of Northumberland. The distance is two and a half miles, and it is necessary to take off shoes and stockings, for the water on the sands will often be six inches deep. A row of posts marks the way, and some of them have ladders, reaching up to a barrel on the top, so that any caught by the tide can find a safe harbour wherein they will suffer nothing more serious than a long wait ! The island is inhabited by fishing folk, living simple healthy lives. There are fine rocks and splendid sands; beautiful flowers and lovely shells. The sea-birds are wonderful. The ruins of the old Cathedral and castle are very interesting. It is a delightful old-world place, out of the rush and hurry of modern life.

Retracing our steps to the mainland, and proceeding westward for a dozen or so miles as the crow flies, we reach the River Till, and the field of Flodden. Here we are near to the big wild wall of the Cheviot hills, and to keep on the English side of the border we need to turn due south. It is then about thirty miles of rough walking through these grandly rugged hills before we come to the field of Otterburn.

But we realise in that walk how it was that the district produced and still produces a hardy race of hunters and sheep-farmers, and why it is that the towns and farms nestle in the valleys, so that the Borderers, when they meant to say, "Rouse the neighbourhood," used the phrase, "Raise the *water*" (meaning, of course, the houses along the waterside). Further south, still going among splendid shaggy hills, we reach the North Tyne River, and soon afterwards some highly interesting Roman remains, including the arches of a fine bridge over the river at the Roman Station of Cilurnum, near Chollerford. This is on the Roman Wall, which has already been described under the heading of Thirlwall. A few miles to the west would bring us to the picturesque but little-known Northumberland Lakes, where the wild swans nest. If we continue south and south-west we can follow the beautiful valleys of the Allan or the South Tyne. This is a district of hills, roads, and castles; the domain of the fated Lord Derwentwater was near here. For beauty the whole of this neighbourhood would be hard to beat; yet it is too little known.

If we still go south, the scenery grows wilder and wilder as we approach the huge mountain of Cross Fell. We may cross into south-east Cumberland and visit the quaint old town of Alston, one of the highest towns in England. Here were once the royal silver mines, when English coins were made from Alston silver. Lead is chiefly mined there now, and the mines are worth a visit. Near Cross Fell also is a rough road called the "Maiden Way," and an old legend says it was made by women, who carried the stones in their aprons! The western slope of the Fell is famous for a specially violent wind called the "Helm wind," which rages there at certain seasons. It is just as if it were rushing fiercely down the hill, with a roaring noise and strength enough to overturn a horse and cart, and to beat the grass and grain till it is black! But though it does a deal of damage it is very exhilarating, making people feel merry in spite of themselves. And on Cross Fell slopes can be seen the beautiful River Tees, which can be followed to its grand waterfalls of the the Cauldron and the High Force. In the first the water dashes on to huge rocks, and is thrown back on itself, roaring, foaming, and fighting; in the second, it tumbles sheer down a dark and noble cliff. And everywhere on the heights there are splendid views.

In making any such excursions as the ones here outlined, into the out-of-the-way parts of Northumberland and the Borders, we find an added pleasure in the character of the people. The Borderers are still a grand race; big men, vigorous, honest, courteous, hospitable, free from all that is mean and small. In some districts you can hear "thou" and "thee" still used, and meet old men who have never seen a railway. One dear old farmer, a real picture of a simple honest man, hearing I had come from London, asked me if the London men had got their hay-crop in yet! One typical Northumbrian, of great natural intelligence, bearing a name famous on the Borders, is station-master at a local station that stands in a wood, and between trains, studies bird and wild-flower till he has made himself a most interesting naturalist. A stranger who has lost his way will find these courteous folk ready to walk a mile or two with him, out of their own way, just to set him right; and he who is tired and hungry will be invited to step in and eat, and perhaps find himself introduced to all the family and treated like an honoured guest; then, not a penny of payment taken, they will set him on his way with a bunch of the best flowers from the garden! For hearts on the Border are very human and warm. So that in due time he who knows the Borderers will delight to hear the unmistakeable Northumbrian or the pronounced Border accent. And he will say to himself: Splendid is the Border scenery, and stirring are the Border ballads, but best of all are the Border men.